HOW MAN~~AGE~~~~S~~ ~~D~~EVELOP MANAGERS

How Managers Can Develop Managers

Alan Mumford

Gower

Published 1993 in hardback by Gower Publishing. Reprinted 1995.

Paperback edition published 1997 by
Gower Publishing
Gower House
Croft Road
Aldershot
Hampshire GU11 3HR
England

Gower
Old Post Road
Brookfield
Vermont 05036
USA

British Library Cataloguing in Publication Data

Mumford, Alan
  How Managers Can Develop Managers
  I. Title
  658

Library of Congress Cataloguing in Publication Data

Mumford, Alan
  How managers can develop managers / Alan Mumford.
    p.   cm.
  Includes bibliographical references.
  1. Executives—Training of. 2. Executive ability. I. Title.
HD38.2M853   1993   93–2292
658.4'07124—dc20   CIP

ISBN 0–566–07403–6 Hbk
     0–566–08009–5 Pbk

Typeset in 10pt Palatino by Photoprint, Torquay, S. Devon and printed in Great Britain at the University Press, Cambridge

Very few are wise by their own counsel, or learned by their own teaching. For he that was only taught by himself had a fool for his master.

Ben Jonson

Contents

List of charts

List of figures

Preface

Most managers accept that they have a responsibility for developing not only themselves, but others. In this book I aim to show how they can carry out this responsibility more effectively by helping to identify the actions they can undertake to help managerial colleagues learn. I do this by describing the circumstances in which learning opportunities can arise or be created, and the practices and behaviours necessary to convert learning opportunities into learning.

The book emphasizes learning from experience at work – through the demands of the job, from problems and opportunities, from bosses, mentors and colleagues. The conversion of the frequently accidental and disorganized ways in which managers have learned when they talk about 'learning from experience' into a more disciplined approach to learning from experience has the greatest potential for improving the development of managers.

The Reader

The book has been designed as a workbook for managers themselves, not a guide for management development specialists to undertake their work. The implications for such specialists are examined in the Appendix.

The Manager as Developer of Others

Of course, each individual is responsible for his or her own development, in the sense that no-one else can do the learning for them. But an effective helping manager providing opportunity, encouragement and time will create a better environment for self-development.

The Structure of the Book

Managers will be better able to help the development of others if they understand fully their own experiences of learning from others. The book therefore proceeds in each chapter through self-analysis and self-discovery by the manager developer, as a necessary precursor to assisting in the development of others.

The book starts where most managers are, by looking at what mangers do as the basis for showing how this work stimulates and requires learning. It then moves on to review what goes into effective learning, before turning to a detailed account of the ways in which managers can help others to learn. The increased understanding which these chapters give managers about how they can help others is then used as the basis for self-development for the manager developer. The final chapter assesses the contribution all these processes will make to the creation of an effective Learning Organization.

Further Reading

As this is not an academic book, and to avoid duplication of references in several chapters, appropriate further reading is given at the end of the book.

Further Information

The material in this book derives mainly from my own experiences, but in some places I have used or referred to the work of others. I should be glad to hear from anyone who wants more information, or who may have experiences or ideas of their own to offer.

Alan Mumford
37 Nightingale Lane
London SW12 8SY

Acknowledgements

The first person to demonstrate by his personal involvement with me how managers develop managers was my boss at John Laing, Don Stradling.

One of the starting points for this book was the work I was encourage to undertake by my colleagues at International Management Centres, and my clients at MCB University Press.

My friend and colleague, Peter Honey, helped me to improve the book.

AM

Introduction

This book is about the contribution that can be made by a manager to the development of others.

> 'He is a terrific manager. He used a lot of positive reinforcement. He was always very approachable. When I had to come to him for something I needed help with he never made me embarrassed.' (From *Breaking the Glass Ceiling* by A.M. Morrison, R.P. White, E. van Velsor, Addison Wesley, 1987)

While most opportunities for helping with development will be created by a manager's boss, others can also be involved too:

> 'I took over responsibility in my company for dealing with work in Southern Africa. I was somewhat uncertain of my steps because I had never worked there or really been involved in it. I went into a meeting to discuss a quite different subject, mentioned my new responsibility, and found a colleague there who had previously held responsibility in that area. He immediately gave me some very helpful hints on what my first actions should be.'

> 'My boss arrived in my office at 8.30 one Tuesday morning: "I've been thinking more about that problem with Client Y you raised with me yesterday. I think it might mean not just a specific problem with that client, but something that runs across several. If you can clear your diary for two hours from 9.00 on Friday, why don't we get together and review what the issues are and the options are for resolving them? You draw up the agenda – you tell me what you want us to tackle, and how I might help".'

> 'The thing about (Subordinate X) was that although he did not have much experience, he had one of the best analytical minds I've come across. But as well as analysing other people's ideas he was pretty creative himself. Best of all, he was very skilled at offering himself in either of these two ways. He avoided the great fault of some bright young people, who don't recognize the difference between being bright and influencing someone. Now I think of it I learned as much from the way he put his ideas across as I did from their content.'

1

'Jean, an interesting opportunity is coming up in Department A. How would you feel about my putting in a word for you? How would it relate to your ideas on your future career? Do you know any of the people there?'

These cases could be multiplied, of course, thousands of times – they are examples of how one manager has been helped by another. In sequence the four examples show help being offered by a colleague, by a boss, by a subordinate and by a mentor. (Although in the last case, the person offering the help might not have seen himself as a mentor in the formal sense.)

Another Perspective

Another set of experiences can be seen initially not so much from the perspective of the person offering help, but on the situations in which help might be necessary.

Manager G has just been promoted from Deputy to full Manager of Purchasing. She attends a meeting to discuss actions to be taken following a downturn in achieved Sales. The different views of Marketing, Sales, Production and Finance are presented at the meeting. Each makes a strong case for the particular line of action each wants to follow.

A customer phones with a quality problem arising from a recently delivered major batch of goods. They want the supplier to send their most senior Production Manager, together with the Quality Manager, to see the reality of the problem on the customer's side. The Production Manager decides to take with him a graduate trainee, 'just to keep your eyes open and take a few notes for us'.

A company has an opportunity to expand its activities by changing from exports from the UK to the provision of services direct in Continental Europe. The Finance Director in charge of the project has worked his way up the organization over a 15-year period which has never included considerable borrowings from the bank, nor dealt with a substantial change in the company's operations.

As a result of the UK Government's policy of devolving managerial control within the UK Civil Service, it has set up a new agency outside the previously normal reporting relationships (i.e. to the Permanent Secretary). A young but 'high flying' Civil Servant currently responsible for an important area of policy within the department is moved to run the agency – which amongst other managerial issues has a staff of 7000 people.

Combining for Effective Development

Two essential elements for effective development are the willingness of individuals to help each other, and the vast variety of situations in which it is possible to learn from managerial work. Up to a point these are combined – people do learn from each other, and they do recognize opportunities within the managerial experiences which are on offer. Unfortunately most managers have a limited ability to recognize opportunities, help and understand the most effective learning processes involved.

There are two prime reasons for this. The first is that managers have rarely been encouraged to pay any attention to the ways in which they learn. The common cliché is that they have 'learned from experience'. In the past they were often not encouraged to understand, interpret or improve their understanding of what that experience involved or meant. The second reason is that until relatively recently in the history of formal management development, management development schemes, systems and programmes have been either inappropriate or ineffective or both. When it became clear that 'learning from experience', however true in principle, often produced managers incapable of doing the work required of them, formal management development processes were identified as the answer. Schemes to take people through an apparently planned sequence of development, with movement from one job to another, were designed. Courses ranging from one or two days on specific skills to two years on the high peaks of an MBA programme were developed as answers to the demand for greater knowledge or skill. All too often the process of management development seemed to remove from managers the motivation either to act on their own behalf or to assist responsibly in the development of others. In the United Kingdom the two great attempts to change this approach were through Self-Development and Action Learning. In their different ways, both concepts recognized that most management development occurs within or around the manager's job. In the case of Action Learning, it is proposed that development should arise from real managerial activities, not through knowledge centred processes for learning off-the-job.

While much formal management development has at least embraced the principles of using real managerial work, a large part of the necessary action has not been effectively tackled. The third element in the triangle of effectiveness, along with the situation and the people, is a recognition of the processes of learning which need to be engaged if the marriage of situation and person is to be productive. Part of that process is the learning sequence itself – a recognition that simply providing someone with an opportunity does not guarantee learning. Another crucial part of the learning process is detailed and dedicated attention to the capacity of individuals to provide help.

The Aim of this Book

The prime purpose for this book is to describe how situation, the potential helper and learning processes can effectively be put together. Moreover, because I choose to focus on real work activities, the concentration is on the line manager, not on the professional developer, as helper. It is indeed yet another manifestation of the failure of much formal management development to grasp the real issues over the last twenty years that there is no book which surveys the totality of the way in which one manager could go about helping another to learn (contrast this with a number of books available for trainers on how to carry out their role).

In making my comments almost entirely about the line manager as helper, I am fully aware of the irony that I nonetheless expect that much of this material will be presented by developers and trainers. However, the irony is more apparent than real. Or at least it is, if my professional colleagues in education, training and development accept that they have two different kinds of responsibility. They, of course, need to provide professional services as the developers of others in a direct sense. They must design effective formal management development schemes, design and run good courses, and provide effective counselling, guidance and help to managers on a variety of issues. But they must recognize that these relationships, powerful and important though they are sometimes for the managers involved, are relatively fleeting and temporary.

The people who can help managers most of the time with their development processes are those around them at work. Therefore the second responsibility of the professional developer and trainer is to help managers carry out their direct helping work more effectively.

The Dominance of Task

One of the reasons why courses are now available on the development of managerial skills, rather than learning such skills from real work experience, is the dominance of task in the real work situation. Most managers have an understandable, if occasionally over-frantic, concern to achieve their managerial goals. For most of them these managerial goals of profit, service and elegantly written policy statements inspire the occasionally violent energy with which managers carry out their work, and the intellectual ingenuity with which many of them perform. However, that energy and drive can be concentrated purely on the task. One of the problems about learning from experience, of reviewing it, articulating it, registering what it means and improving it, is that it is always at best a secondary feature of what a manager has been doing. Moreover, though it may be second, it is second by a very long distance. One of the reasons why courses were invented was to change the priority – to create circumstances in which learning was the prime task and managing, if it was involved at all, was a secondary feature.

In this book I am deliberately challenging the suggestion that the managerial focus on the task itself, which I accept in the real work situation will always be primary, cannot be effectively supplemented by well designed learning through and around the job. It is my experience that managers can be intrigued and stimulated by finding ways in which real work and learning can be combined. What I am offering after all is a recognition that some of their deeply held beliefs about the virtues of learning from experience are actually valid. Unfortunately, some of my colleagues in the training and education world have too often behaved, if they have not spoken, as if learning from experience was a low value, low intellectual challenge, low productivity exercise.

Why Develop Others?

There are five reasons why managers develop others:

- They pursue the resolution of problems and in the process accidentally aid the development of others.
- They believe that improving the performance of others will reflect favourably on their own individual performance and perhaps also create more space for their own managerial interests and ambitions.
- They derive personal satisfaction from helping someone to grow.
- They develop their own skills, knowledge and insight as a result of sharing experiences with others.
- Their organization demands that they do, through formal management development systems such as Appraisal and Succession Plans.

The order of these reasons reflects their significance to most managers. The problem with many formal management development schemes is that they assume that the fifth reason given above is the most powerful – and that they further assume that the development activities are those that can be defined and recorded through formal systems such as Appraisal or a course on Principles of Management. The premise of this book is instead that managers will develop others primarily because it suits their own interests.

The Principle of Reciprocity

The idea that managers will help develop other managers because it is often in their own interests to do so can be taken further. The relationship involved is not primarily that of teacher/student, with the giving by one person and receiving by another. It can often be a mutually beneficial relationship, in which the participants both give and receive. It is a relationship which, when developed, becomes one of partnership and dialogue. The guiding force can be the Principle of Reciprocity, under which managers recognize that assisting in the development of others is not one-way traffic undertaken for the benefit of others, but a reciprocal activity beneficial to both parties.

Self-discovery, Self-development

A manager cannot develop someone else; the title of this book is a convenient shorthand. An individual's development can be enhanced by an effective helping manager, providing opportunity, encouragement and time. The structure of the book is built on self-analysis and self-discovery by the helping manager as a necessary precursor to assisting in the development of others. Passages of description and suggestions for action are therefore accompanied by exercises for the manager.

A Rose by Another Name?

The word 'learner' is used throughout. This has the merits of accuracy, consistency, acceptability and generalizability.

Accuracy We concentrate on individuals who in a variety of situations, through a diversity of methods and a collection of individuals are assisted to learn.

Consistency Some people may wish to differentiate between 'learning' and 'development'. This distinction is not one which most managers find helpful.

Acceptability Learners are sometimes called mentees, protégés or coachees. These words are cumbersome and give no clear indication of what is going on. The purpose of the relationship is not to be a protégé or coachee (words which anyway have a flavour of being wholly subordinate in the process). The purpose is to acquire learning.

Generalizability The use of the word learners not only avoids specialist terms such as mentee. It also focuses on the general and consistent role – learner – rather than the specific and temporary role of coachee, protégé.

PART I
HOW MANAGERS LEARN

1

What managers do

In order to use real managerial work as a vehicle for learning, we have to understand it. One of the most helpful things that can be offered to a manager, therefore, is an opportunity to review what the job is, why it is like that and how it is to be performed most effectively. There are still organizations, particularly small or newly formed, or in the professions or service activities, where no kind of statement of managerial role or purpose exists. In most organizations there will be a formal statement, itself a reflection of some kind of organizational and managerial history. Very often these statements and the cultural views of what a manager should do are themselves the result of layers of sometimes only partially understood or integrated theory and practice concerned with 'what managerial work is all about'. Some of that theory and articulated practice may also be based on experiences and views of years ago – a management course attended, a big consultancy exercise, a need to establish job descriptions for salary purposes.

Understanding the Present from the Past

There are five stages in the evolution of thought about what managers do:

1. The Generalization Stage

The so-called classical theorists like Fayol and his successors, such as Urwick and Brech and many subsequent imitators, offered a set of prescriptive statements about how managers should carry out their work. These amounted to:

- forecast and plan
- organize
- motivate
- coordinate
- control.

They presumed that effective managerial processes were essentially the same for all managers in all kinds of organizations. In that sense, though in that sense alone, they were similar to another set of generalizers. These offered large-scale statements of personality traits. This was essentially the 'great man' school of management, presuming that managers achieved what they did through force of personality expressed through such concepts as leadership, initiative, and 'getting the chaps to work with you'.

2.   The Scientific Stage

In the 1950s and 1960s the classical view was challenged by a view of management as a wholly rational and scientific process. Although the components of the scientific process were not necessarily agreed or integrated, Operations Research, Decision Making Theory and Human Behaviour in Organizations became important elements in what was taught, at least, in management schools.

3.   The Management by Objectives Stage

In the 1960s, both in the United Kingdom and in the United States, the main thrust was towards results. Instead of describing what managers did, or how they did it, the MBO process concentrated on clarity of definition of objectives, key results, targets.

4.   The Contingency/Realistic Stage

From the 1960s until relatively recently, the temptation to generalize about what 'all managers ought to do' has been attacked by a series of research studies, again in both the United Kingdom and the United States. Perhaps the most powerful names associated with this have been Burns and Stalker, Lawrence and Lorsch, Rosemary Stewart, Henry Mintzberg and John Kotter. I describe this as the Contingent or Realist School because their detailed studies, often by observation of managers in a variety of settings, show differences in how managers operate. Not only do they do things in a different way depending on the particular organizational requirements or setting, but they actually need to do so.

5.   The Competency Stage

Led by the innovative work of Richard Boyatzis in the United States, the Competency Stage has involved an attempt to define what managers have to do well. In many respects reminiscent of the earlier attempts to define management skills, competences often embrace more than skill, and include aspects of personality. While Boyatzis offered a broad sweep view of competences found in several thousand managers, the Competency approach was subsequently developed to be more compatible with Contingency Theory so that organizations developed their own list of competences. In the United Kingdom that approach in turn has changed direction, with generalized national competences developed and promoted under the Management Charter Initiative.

From the point of view of the present book there are at least three significant implications of this historical analysis. The first is that at least until the advent of the qualification centred Management Charter Initiative competences in the UK, the shift in our understanding of what managers do has been towards specificity and contingency and therefore greater reality, rather than towards generalization. Only at the highest, most abstract and most useless level of generalization is it possible to talk about 'what all managers do'. In terms of helping managers to do their jobs more effectively this will not be a surprise to most practising managers. In their real world, grappling with day-to-day problems, they do see differences in the job that one does as compared with another. You only have to talk to a sales manager in an organization and then to a production director (usually not down the corridor, but in a separate building) to find out that this is true. It is only in the context of courses and books that managers are encouraged to generalize and 'see how much they have in common with each other'. While this has merit for discussion purposes, it has very little advantage in terms of helping with the specific aspects of the individual manager's job and learning requirements.

The second point worth recognizing is that it is desirable to keep a certain sceptical distance from any new statement about what managers do. When it is suggested that we have 'finally' identified the distinctive characteristics of management, and learning plans should be associated with that new statement, we should remember the previous 'answer', also presented with the fervour drawn from belief.

The third point is that while each wave of analysis has added to the total conceptual understanding of the manager's job, attempts to integrate all these various perspectives have not been successful at either the academic or practical level. One of the many paradoxes about management is that it is, in most organizations, a complex activity, yet attempts to describe that complexity, to ensure that individual managers recognize each interrelationship in a complex structure of systems, networks, competing objectives, are unlikely to be helpful in the day-to-day managerial world. Of course, this can be attempted, and up to a point done, in the time available on a full-time two-year MBA programme. However, one is bound to ask how much of this complex analysis remains for MBAs when they return to or enter the managerial world.

This book is written from a Contingent/Realist viewpoint. Generalizations about all managers lead to inaccurate and therefore unhelpful views of the work of particular managers, and of their most important development needs. Any approach to helping the development of other managers is therefore best based on specific discussion of 'what does your job really involve?', not on a generalized list.

A View of the Reality of Management

Some picture needs to be created, avoiding both complexity and oversimplification. The one I use, combining the findings of researchers and my own experience as a manager, business school tutor and researcher, is shown in Figure 1.1. The figure reflects issues which are fundamental to the approach suggested in this book. While I would not go as far as Tom Peters in emphasizing the extent to which management could be described as chaotic,

---

Hectic Pace

Fragmented Work Patterns

Turbulent Work Environment – Dynamic

Behaviour

Is More	**Is Less**
Intuitive	Rational
Responsive	Reflective
Unaware	Sensitive
Unplanned	Proactive

Processing Information – Often Unprogrammed

Full In-Tray – both Physical and Mental

Use of Informal Networks

Interactive – with Systems and People

Multi-Programmed

More Often Constrained than Innovative

Varies according to

- nature of job
- perceptions and preferences of individual

Figure 1.1 Reality of management

there are elements of turbulence and hectic decision making in swiftly changing circumstances. Managers learn to cope with these circumstances partly using their own reflective intelligence, partly by observation of skills of others, partly by sharing issues and problems with colleagues, mentors and bosses.

While our purpose clearly must be to increase the amount of reflective intelligence applied by all of these participants in the learning process, the solution is not simply to state the requirements that managers should somehow become more rational, more thoughtful and more aware of issues and their surroundings. While these are often very desirable characteristics, to assert their desirability in relation to a process – learning – which has low priority and reward for most of them is not likely to be immediately attractive. We must try to enable managers to operate at an incremental level by adding a little more thought, a little more planning and a little more care to their developmental relationships and therefore to their learning capacity, rather than asking them to transform themselves into marvellous exemplars of learning. For most managers most of the time, task will be predominant; therefore our job is somehow to engage their attention to a greater degree on some aspects of process for part of the time. We need to recognize that we are challenging the unplanned, reflexive but often highly effective managerial styles of many of those with whom we deal.

When we have achieved progress at this incremental level, with individuals or groups of managers, then we can propose more challenging approaches in which learning is highlighted as a main purpose of the managerial activity.

Opportunism and Structured Development

The struggle in management development has for thirty years centred on providing processes felt to be more effective than those that managers normally use when they talk about learning from experience. As a consequence many formal management development schemes are based on highly tailored statements of what managers should do and depend on detailed training needs analyses carried out via interviews, repertory grids, job descriptions, analysis of objectives and priorities from the business plan. These can all be appropriate contributors to the kind of structured management development which many human resource directors, management development advisers and management educators would recognize and favour. A later part of this book is concerned with how to use such processes, and how the responsibilities of bosses and mentors can be related to these structured processes.

However, if Figure 1.1 is an accurate reflection of what many managers do, the fully structured approach will cater for only part of the managerial world – that part of it which can be defined, structured in advance and used to direct development needs. The unplanned part of the manager's world is at risk of being ignored and not catered for, or, worse, recognized and 'replaced' by some formal process. Management development must take more account of both formal and informal processes and clearly any suggestions we make for those people who help in the development of others must also cater for both informal and formal processes. We must equip managers not only to be effective mentors or bosses in the formal context of a structured management development scheme, with neat statements of responsibilities and plans for who does what, with whom, when. We also need to enable managers to take up exactly those responsibilities through their normal work activities, possibly without ever involving the management development and personnel specialists.

Because most opportunities for development occur on the job and are currently unplanned, Chapters 2 and 3 deal with opportunities which can be recognized in the work managers do, but which exist outside the formal management development system.

EXERCISE 1.1

1. In your own experience of management development, to what extent do you think you have learned from informal and unplanned experiences around the job, as compared with structured experiences through a formal management development process (e.g. Succession Planning or courses).
2. To what extent do you think that it is possible to generalize about 'what managers do'? Who has the most similar job to yourself within your organization? Who has the most dissimilar job? What are the similarities/ dissimilarities you encounter with managers you meet from other organizations?
3. Think of a boss, colleague or subordinate and his or her attitude to management. What differences do you identify in their views, compared with your own?

2

Management and learning

Managers acquire their views about what they have to do in their jobs from a variety of sources. The previous chapter indicated some of the stages involved in this. Now we turn to some views on the ways in which ideas about managerial work are described, such as knowledge, skill, attitudes and competence. Then we can consider how the things that managers do provide the basis not only for what managers need to learn but for how they learn it. In doing so, clearer understanding of the principle that managers 'learn from experience' will emerge.

We need to remember first the paradox about the nature of managerial work and learning from it. Learning from day-to-day activities is not only the most prevalent process; it is probably for most people the most important. It is also the least disciplined, the most subject to competing time pressures, as compared with the more dedicated learning processes offered off the job. While learning from real work has the potential to offer tremendous productivity benefits, actual achievement is at a much lower level than it could be and needs to be.

What Job am I Doing?

The work a manager actually does derives primarily from the interplay of the following factors:

- The objective demands of the job;
- The particular context in which the job is being performed;
- The personal priorities, skills and knowledge of the job holder;
- Immediate and pressing claims on the manager for attention and action.

15

A more detailed view of influences on what managers do is given in Figure 2.1.

The net result of all the influences on what a manager does, in terms of learning from the job, is a constant pressure to return to the demands of the task. Managers who are trying to help others are doubly caught by this tendency. If they have relatively little time they are prepared to dedicate to thinking through their own learning requirements, the amount of time they are willing to dedicate to others is likely to be less. While not wholly true – because sometimes more senior people will accept wider responsibility for others – it is an important point that we look at in Chapters 9 and 10 where we consider formal processes through which managers help others.

Managers generally are not self-analytical. Nor are they prone to regular reviews of what they are doing and how they are doing it, unless they are jogged through an Appraisal scheme or through some other process requiring them to review their work. The formal elements of management development tend to take managers through a neat process of job definition, skill requirement and development needs. Outside these structured methods managers operate according to their understanding of priorities for their work, undertake managerial activities to meet those priorities, and learn from this as a consequence. While in principle every hour of the day could be seen as presenting some kind of learning opportunity, most managers do not recognize the opportunity – which is of course one of the areas in which they can be helped by others. Learning from real work activities therefore tends to be partial, insufficient, inefficient, poorly understood and badly integrated. By badly integrated I mean that particular items of learning acquired are often not properly compared with similar incidents or with equivalent functional requirements. Here is an example:

> A manager was discussing what he had learned recently from a series of selection interviews he had conducted as part of a recruitment exercise. He said that he had learned from experience that it was much better to conduct interviews with most people in a relatively relaxed and informal style. He did not believe in the effectiveness of a hard-edged, inquisitorial approach. This manager was also involved in selecting a consultant to carry out some work concerned with Information Technology. He was asked what similarities or differences he saw between selection interviewing and interviewing a prospective consultant. He replied that he had not thought about it – he had seen them as totally different.

Of course managers do sometimes review what they are doing, how they are doing it and even why they are doing it. Outside formal review processes these reflections occur usually because of some external circumstance such as:

- A change in the demand for the service or product offered
- A change in organizational structure
- Acquiring a new boss
- Acquiring new responsibilities

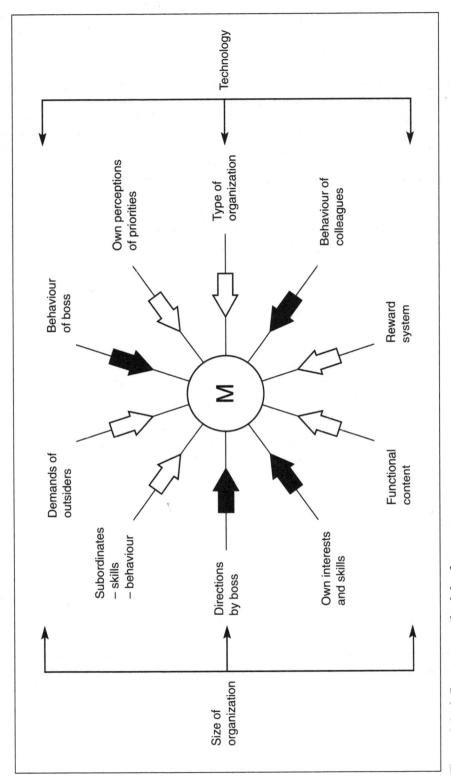

Figure 2.1 Influences on the job of a manager

- Moving to a new job.

Even when this occurs managers rarely follow through the complete sequence of events which would enable them to construct effective learning. Largely this is because no-one will have suggested to them that such a sequence with an end purpose called 'learning' is actually desirable. It is precisely such a suggestion and help with such a sequence which is, of course, one of the roles of the helper. Most particularly even where managers have undertaken some review of what their job is all about, they tend not to work to some model or framework which would enable them to understand the new or changed knowledge or skill requirements in the job. The kind of words which they will, however, tend to use, probably derive from the more formal Training Needs Analysis System:

- knowledge
- skills
- attitude.

Some large organizations, particularly in the United Kingdom, have taken up the word 'Competence' and this has now become a significant element of the UK Management Charter Initiative. Because this is very much a formally structured method of defining managerial requirements, and has become the working method towards a managerial qualification, it is dealt with in Chapter 9. This chapter also embraces all the other ways of defining what are usually called Training Needs but which preferably should be called Learning Needs, through a formal management development system.

Knowledge, Skills, Insight

I have carried out two research projects on how directors learn to do their work as directors. In the first project my colleagues and I looked at the balance of contribution between formal management development processes such as Succession Planning, job rotation and courses, as compared with what we described as informal and accidental learning experiences – the subject of this chapter. Our second research activity took up the familiar statement that 'we learned from experience', and looked in detail at the ways in which the directors we studied actually learned. The results of our investigation concern what managers learned, how they learned it and what help was available to them in learning. Here are three examples of what people learned:

'I had the job of setting up a major expansion for my company. It involved identifying a new site onto which we could expand. This meant going into all the issues about best location in terms of price, transport, availability of people, where the customers were, where it should be in relation to our existing business.'

'I was very impressed with the way he chaired the meeting. I tend to take the lead a lot but I saw he was at least as effective as I am in a much more subtle approach to drawing out and clarifying views.'

'People can and do act differently at conferences. Sometimes the jokers become very serious, and quite unexpected people pop up with new ideas. It made me think of other situations in which people's behaviour alters.'

In our analysis we saw these as respectively Knowledge, Skills and Insight. We found in our analysis of the hundreds of items presented to us that Insight was a more helpful categorization than Attitude. Not only are there arguments about the extent to which Attitude can be changed, for example through formal training, but we found the concept of Insight much more applicable to current or prospective learning – attitudes often, of course, go back a long way!

When do Managers Learn from Experience?

There are at least three different answers to this question. One answer as already suggested is that managers learn when faced with new demands and new circumstances. Think of the Civil Servant being moved from a policy role to an executive agency, the manager moved from Marketing into a direct Sales role or the industrial relations specialist moved into a training and development role. That is one answer to the large scale issue of when people learn.

A second answer is that they learn when they encounter a particular kind of experience – meeting a new customer, visiting a manufacturing plant, negotiating with a new supplier.

A third answer is that people actually carry out their learning at different times in the managerial activity. For many, learning is something acquired through a managerial activity but recognized subsequently. In our research we found that the timing of learning and some parts of the process involved in it could be usefully described in a model we called 'The Four Approaches'. We found that the ways in which directors described how and when they learned could be summarized as in Figure 2.2 (see p. 20).

The details of the four approaches are as follows.

1.   The Intuitive Approach

The Intuitive Approach involves learning from experience, but not through a conscious process. The person using the Intuitive Approach claims that learning is an inevitable consequence of having experiences. If questioned, he

---

THE FOUR APPROACHES

- Intuitive
- Incidental
- Retrospective
- Prospective

Figure 2.2   Learning from experience on the job

or she is able to talk in detail about a variety of different experiences describing what happened and what was achieved. The learning or developmental aspects are rarely, if ever, referred to. Indeed, the Intuitive Approach sees managing and good business practices as synonymous with learning. Someone using the Intuitive Approach, therefore, finds it difficult, and unnecessary, to articulate what they learned or how they learned it. They are content that learning occurs through some natural process of osmosis.

Typical comments by users of this approach are: 'I'm sure I'm learning all the time but I can't be more specific.' 'I just do it but I can't tell you how.' 'I do that already without calling it learning.' 'I suspect you are doing it all the time without realizing you're doing so.'

Since people using the Intuitive Approach put their trust in learning as a 'natural', effortless process they find it difficult to accept that there are advantages to be gained by making the process more deliberate and conscious, either for themselves or for other people.

2.   The Incidental Approach

The Incidental Approach involves learning by chance from activities that jolt an individual into conducting a 'post mortem'. A variety of incidents can act as jolts but common ones are when something out of the ordinary crops up or where something has not gone according to plan. Mishaps and frustrations often provide the spur.

When something makes an impression on people using the Incidental Approach they are inclined to mull over what happened in an informal, unstructured way. They may do this in odd moments such as while travelling between appointments or home from work, or in the bath. People using Incidental Learning tend to use the benefit of hindsight as a way of rationalizing, even justifying, what happened. As a result, they may jot something down 'for the record', but not in the form of learning points, more as an insurance in case, subsequently, they need to cover themselves.

Typical comments by users of this approach are: 'I learn from the unfamiliar parts of my job, not from the bits I am already familiar with and have already mastered.' 'If you know how to do something you aren't going to learn from it.' 'It's the originality of the experience that provokes more reflection.' 'You *only* learn from your mistakes.'

People using the Incidental Approach often find it easier to conduct their post mortems by talking things over with someone else, preferably someone who was also present during the experience in question.

3. The Retrospective Approach

The Retrospective Approach involves learning from experience by looking back over what happened and reaching conclusions about it. In common with the Incidental Approach, the Retrospective Approach is especially provoked by mishaps and mistakes. In addition, however, people using this approach are more inclined to draw lessons from routine events and successes. They therefore extract learning from a diverse range of small and large, positive and negative experiences.

People using the Retrospective Approach conduct reviews, sometimes in their heads, sometimes in conversation and sometimes on paper. The sequence looks like this:

Something has happened	→	It is reviewed	→	Conclusions are reached

The outcome in the Retrospective Approach is that considered conclusions are reached. An individual, by reviewing, acquires knowledge, skills and insights or has them confirmed and reinforced. Skills-based courses often provide opportunities for conscious Retrospective Learning – though the opportunities are not always used properly.

Typical comments by users of this approach are: 'It helps to hold things up to the light.' 'Reviewing is essential to put thoughts into perspective.' 'You never really understand something until you write it down.'

4. The Prospective Approach

The Prospective Approach involves all the Retrospective elements but includes an additional dimension. Whereas Retrospection concentrates on reviewing what happened after an experience, the Prospective Approach includes planning to learn before an experience. Future events are seen, not merely as things to be done which are important in their own right, but also as opportunities to learn. Individuals using this approach are learners who are constantly alert to the possibility of learning from a whole variety of experiences.

In the event, what the individual expected to learn may not materialize quite as planned. But the process of thinking about learning in advance makes it likely that they will extract some learning from the situation rather than drawing a blank.

The sequence in Prospective Learning is:

| Plan to learn | → | Implement the plan | → | Review the plan | → | Reach conclusions |

Again, courses provide clear opportunities for this approach, but there are often weaknesses in implementation.

Typical comments by users of this approach are: 'I learn because I go there expecting to do so.' 'There is no substitute for thorough planning, not only to get things done but also to learn from doing them.' 'Sorting out what you want to achieve in advance increases your chances of getting something worthwhile.'

The Four Approaches model is one way for managers to test their own preferred approach to learning from experience, and therefore to assess how they are likely to help others learn from their experiences.

Improved Learning From Experience

A number of elements must be present to improve the way in which individuals learn from experience. They need to be given, or helped to recognize, learning opportunities (see next chapter). They need to understand their preferred way of learning – the idea of learning styles. They need to understand that any learning experience involves the four stages of the Learning Cycle (see Chapter 4 for more on Styles and Cycle). The organization in general, and the particular people around the learner have to be sympathetic to, and provide rewards for, learning. This chapter has centred on how the particular activities in which a manager is involved can generate the need for, and the occasion of, learning and development.

When managers talk about learning from experience, and certainly when they are asked to review their experiences in any kind of depth, it quickly becomes apparent that not only is there a wide range of activities from which they have learned, but that they rarely have learned as much as they could have done. The development of ideas centred on a more conscious recognition of how activities can be seen as learning opportunities is fundamental to what managers can do to help their own learning, and that of others.

We found in our research that most directors had not developed for themselves any process by which they understood what they had learned let alone how they had learned it, hence the importance of giving some help through the Knowledge, Skills, Insight categorization and the Four Approaches. Another issue was the extent to which the people involved relied a great deal on their own solitary effort in order to understand their learning. Solitary learning is the most difficult of all processes in terms of real managerial work. It is of course entirely appropriate for the acquisition of knowledge through a book or video or computer software. But most effective learning from managerial activities would be improved if people were able to share, question and confer with other people – which explains the need for this book.

One More Time – Managerial Activities as Triggers

Any managerial activity contains the potential for learning. It might be totally new learning or confirming learning previously acquired or adjusting previous learning, for example 'this technique worked with these people in this situation, but it didn't work when I tried it with someone else'. The list of managerial activities from which people could learn would be endless, and would in any event apply to some people in some circumstances and not in others depending on the relevance of any learning activity to the particular job or project of the managers. With that proviso, some of the triggers for learning are given in Figure 2.3.

A successful piece of work
Working with different people
Being involved in an acquisition or merger
Changed objectives
Changed priorities
Confronting difficult colleagues
Declining profit/Increased targets
Different standards of performance
Deputizing for another manager
Major difficulty
Membership of a working party or task force
New assignment
New challenge
New job
New organization
New project
Problem solving with a new group
Shock or crisis
Using old learning in a new environment
Visiting or working in a new country
Working with a new boss
Working with new colleagues
An unsuccessful piece of work

Figure 2.3   Triggers for learning

EXERCISE 2.1

1. Have there been any recent changes in the priorities of what you do in your job?

2.   What has caused these changes (see page 16)?
3.   Have there, as a result, been changes in knowledge, skill or insight required of you for effective performance?
4.   Have you acquired new knowledge, skills and insight within your job recently?

EXERCISE 2.2

1.   Which of the managerial activities in your job provide the best past learning experience?
2.   Now you have reviewed your job, do you see some activities which might provide good learning experiences in future?
3.   What would you have to do in order to increase your learning from real managerial work?
4.   Who might help you – and in what way?

EXERCISE 2.3

1.   Could you add triggers from your own experience (see Figure 2.3)?
2.   Which have been the most influential in your own learning and development?
3.   Which do you perceive as being potentially most valuable for someone with whom you might have a helping relationship (subordinate, colleague)?

EXERCISE 2.4

1.   Review the Four Approaches to learning from experience.
2.   Which approach do you use most often?
3.   Which approach do you use least often?
4.   Identify a subordinate whose development you are trying to help. Which of the approaches do you think he or she uses most?

3

Opportunities for learning

The aim of this chapter is to show some of the variety of work related activities in which a manager may be involved, and from which learning may be derived. It examines in more detail the propositions about work and learning presented in the previous chapter. It shows how opportunities can be defined and used.

Managers carry out their managerial work in order to achieve managerial purposes. This statement of the obvious is necessary in order to be clear why so often opportunities for learning are not recognized, or if recognized not fully utilized. So important is the managerial purpose that managers will sometimes say that they believe it to be very difficult to learn *consciously* from their managerial work. Fortunately, as this book shows, it is not in fact difficult. One helpful way of assuring managers of this is to ask them to think about the number of factors they actually have to consider when carrying out managerial work.

One of the most frequently quoted managerial activities is decision making. While the prime purpose of an activity may be 'to make a decision', a number of factors contribute to the decision and have to be thought about by the manager. While discussing the facts involved in making a decision, managers will be considering how effectively they are communicating the ideas which it is necessary to communicate. They will have to take into account how to influence other people round the table, and what longer term consequences may be involved. They will reflect on how to 'sell' the eventual decision to other colleagues, boss, subordinates. In fact managers are thinking about a number of different factors at once.

So the view that managers find it very difficult to learn at the same time as they are managing need not be accepted – why should *learning* at the same time as making a decision be seen as more difficult than communicating, influencing and so on?

Indeed, at one level, though admittedly often a superficial one, managers will claim that most of their learning has been secured through experience; they therefore know very well that it is possible to learn from doing. The problem really only arises when we try to articulate what actually needs to go into the learning part of the process. That problem arises because so few managers have had any opportunity to consider the learning process carefully, to understand their own preferences for learning and exactly how to set about utilizing real managerial activities for learning.

The Commuter Train

Anyone who commutes regularly from one place to another by train learns from experience two main points which can make travelling less frustrating and physically wearing. The traveller learns that a difference of five minutes in the time of catching a train may affect the number of other commuters packed into it. Five minutes earlier, or later, than the apparently appropriate time will provide a less physically stressful journey. Secondly, the commuter learns the best position of the carriages – though a choice may have to be based on two different needs. One carriage may be the least packed on arrival at the station. Unfortunately another carriage may be the right one if you want to stop immediately opposite the exit at your final destination. You learn from experience how to balance these factors to produce an outcome which is most acceptable to you.

Learning from Experience at Work

Many learning experiences at work have similar characteristics – learning is often acquired relatively unconsciously by a process normally called 'trial and error', and indeed often involves trade-offs similar to that between physical comfort and time of arrival (i.e. achieved managerial result). The fact that we learn from experience at work is not only recognized by managers but frequently claimed as being either the best way or the only way, or superior to some other process such as going on a course. The misfortune of a great deal of management development since the 1950s has been that the eagerness of personnel and management development specialists to improve what they quite rightly regard as inefficient processes of learning on the job has led them to give far too much priority to replacing learning from experience on the job with other kinds of activity. An alternative incorrect assumption has been that because managers learn from work experience 'naturally', all you need to do is to provide them with more work experiences in order to increase the amount of learning.

In my research, especially with senior managers and directors, I have acquired a substantial volume of evidence to support my own conclusions over thirty years. The fact is that although all managers learn from experience many are unaware *how* they learn and are unclear of the end result.

Long before any recognition of modern managerial techniques Plato said:

'Experience teaches our best flute players. Experience also teaches our worst flute players.'

Perhaps most helpful of all for our purposes here, T.S. Eliot said:

'We had the experience but we missed the meaning.'

Managerial life is replete with opportunities to learn from experience. At its most extreme one could claim that every activity which a manager undertakes provides an opportunity to consider what was done, how it was done and how it could be improved – and from such a task-centred review acquire relevant learning. Such an approach would represent an intolerable burden even for someone dedicated to more effective learning processes. What we need to do is to expand the number of occasions on which managers recognize specific activities as learning opportunities. We also need to assist them with ideas, techniques and checklists which enable them actually to squeeze more learning out of those managerial activities which they now recognize to be learning opportunities.

It seems that managers who:

- become stuck (or plateaued) in their managerial careers,
- begin to slide back down the managerial mountain, or
- are removed for failure to deliver

are those who have had experience but have not recognized its significance. Some managers have an experience and pass on. The effective manager has an experience, learns and moves on. This is the manager Peter Honey and I call 'The Opportunist Learner'.

A great deal of learning at the moment is entirely unconscious and is caused by a reaction to particular problems or events (Intuitive and Incidental). It is one of the necessary features of modern management development that we recognize how far, as illustrated in Chapters 1 and 2, accidental learning is likely to predominate, as suggested in the expression 'that new project will give him a chance to learn'. We need to promote a greater element of consciousness, of reflection, indeed critical reflection, on what has occurred. Even more testing, we need to give people the tools they require to think about opportunities in advance. All too often the attention of managers in learning from experience is centred on failures, difficulties and problems they have had to overcome, often in an unfriendly and unaware organizational environment. We need to help them reduce the pain frequently associated with these occurrences, and instead to increase the amount of pleasure which can be secured from, for example, learning from success as much as learning from difficulty.

Finally we need ways of showing managers that we are describing an attractive double benefit process. To carry out a piece of work, and learn effectively from it, gives two rewards for the price of one piece of managerial work.

Examples of Being Helped to Learn

Over the next few pages we shall consider a vast collection of activities from which it is possible to learn. In this next section we will be concentrating on some examples of managers learning from activities where they were helped to learn by someone else.

Cutting the Budget

The manager of a department calls together his section heads for a meeting early on Monday morning. On Friday lunchtime he had sent a note round to everyone, and had spoken to a few, to say that it was clear they would have a budget problem for the rest of the year. On Monday he started the meeting by explaining that, as several of them knew, their revenue achievement in the first three months of the financial year was 18 per cent below budget. He had talked with the Sales people to see whether this shortfall would be made up in the remaining nine months, and the view was that, although sales would recover to some extent, the existing deficit would not be made up. So he had called everybody together to discuss how they could achieve a substantial cut in costs. He was setting as a realistic target a 20 per cent cut because he felt there should be some margin in case sales did not in fact return to planned level in the remaining nine months.

Jane X, a relatively new section head in Market Research, participated in the discussion. Some section heads were in favour of a simple percentage cut in each section's budget, on the grounds that this was quick, did not need any further discussion and related to the priorities established in the original budget. Others argued that with so large a cut there was a need to review the complete budget, accepting no existing cost elements, i.e. a zero-based budgeting approach. Others found this impractical, but argued that instead of drastic cuts across the board, cuts should be made according to some order of priorities. The ensuing discussion showed that most section heads saw their own work as having high priority.

After a long, and at times very heated, discussion it was agreed that each section head would review the budget for the section on three dimensions. They should establish, however reluctantly, candidates which would add up to a 20 per cent cut in the section's budget. These proposals should be accompanied by a statement on the impact of these cuts and on whether the impact on the work of the department would be short term or long term.

Over lunch after the meeting Jane discussed what had happened with one of her fellow section heads. They thought the departmental manager had handled it extremely well and her colleague actually scribbled on a piece of paper their views as to why the meeting had reached a clear decision and one acceptable to everybody there. They thought the manager had listened very well, had given equal air-time to the section heads including the less vocal, had summarized and clarified so that people could see the advantages and disadvantages of each proposal.

They noticed through this review for the first time that one of the major issues, the short- versus long-term impact, was one which the departmental manager had introduced himself, but almost at the end of the discussion. They discussed why he had not started off with this, if indeed he might have had it in mind at the beginning. They concluded that if he did have it in mind it was a good thing to leave it to the end because it allowed everybody to express their opinions and feel that the outcome was not pre-determined. The end result, anyway, was that the debate had secured commitment to the eventual solution.

This example is interesting from a number of different points of view. In terms of one of the issues presented in this book – formalized development activities compared with managerial activities not originally identified as 'development' – it is of significance. Many management development programmes, especially for middle managers, encourage the concept of coaching (Chapters 6 and 7 cover this). Many managers receive very little coaching after their very early days – if indeed they receive it then. One of the reasons they rarely identify this process is that what management developers are keen to call coaching, managers do not recognize to be going on. What they see is something like the example now understood by Jane and her colleague. Here was an activity which I call mutual problem solving. It does not involve the boss explicitly setting out to improve the problem solving and decision making processes of a group of subordinates or one subordinate – the activity management developers call coaching. Since such problem solving activities are common (though not, of course, always managed as well as in the case quoted) we ought to help managers see that what is involved in them is a development process. In many circumstances it would be better to do this than attempt to persuade them to undertake a discrete activity called 'coaching', which is:

- outside their experience;
- uncomfortable in style and technique for many of them; and,
- for many, seen merely as a development activity and not 'real work'.

Customer Care

The manager of an hotel is called from his office by a receptionist to deal with an angry customer. The customer complains that he has been interrupted in his bedroom three times in the space of half an hour. First of all the cleaner arrived to deal with his room. She responded politely to his request that she return later. However, twenty minutes later there was a knock on the door, the key turned and a woman announcing herself as the housekeeper stepped into the room. She explained that her task was to check that the cleaner had done her work satisfactorily. Ten minutes elapsed after her speedy departure, when there was the third tap on the door. This time a man stood in the doorway and said that he wanted to check the mini-bar.

The customer had arrived at reception, complained about the apparent inefficiency of a process involving three people, and the effect of the interruptions on what he was trying to do – he was writing a report in his room. He had clearly not been satisfied by the receptionist's answer that it was the hotel's policy to carry out the cleaning and the two checking processes before guests checked out as they were asked to do by 11 o'clock in the morning. He asked to see the manager. The manager arrived, taking with him his deputy, since his computer screen in his office had shown that the customer was a senior manager from an organization which frequently used the hotel.

The deputy manager listened while the customer repeated his complaint. The hotel manager, with considerable expressions of sympathy about the disruption, attempted to deal with the complaint. First of all, though with great politeness, he said that it need not have occurred if the occupant had put the 'do not disturb' notice on his room. The room occupant replied sarcastically that he had thought of that too. Unfortunately the notice had been missing when he looked for it, and the housekeeper had failed to replace it before the arrival of the mini-bar attendant. In any event he wanted to discuss why there were three interventions of this kind in such a short time. The hotel manager responded that it was hotel policy that each of the three had their own specific job to do and 'it is, of course, for the good of our customers since it means they have rooms which we know are clean and well looked after'. The room occupant departed still dissatisfied, offering as a parting shot that it seemed clear to him that the whole process was designed to benefit the hotel not their customers.

The hotel manager and his deputy returned to the manager's room. The manager sat behind his desk, blew out his cheeks and asked 'How would you have handled him?'

Project Z

A director, eighteen months from retirement, has been moved out of his last line job to act as 'Director Without Portfolio'. As his first task, the Chief Executive asks him to carry out a SWOT (Strength, Weaknesses, Opportunities, Threats) analysis on the five main activities in the organization. He sets up a project group with representatives chosen by him from five different areas of the organization. As the Finance participant he chooses a young man, not personally known to him, but said by the Director of Finance to be of high potential. He had joined the company a year earlier after completing a prestigious MBA. After the first two meetings of the project group, the Project Director calls in the Finance participant. 'I would just like to talk over what is happening on the group. How do you think things are going?' 'To be honest, a little more slowly than I expected. Some of the people, particularly the Marketing guys, don't seem to understand that all this stuff about customer satisfaction in the end adds up to whether we can afford to finance their ideas.' 'I like a number of aspects of the contribution you are making. There is one point I would like you to think about before the next meeting. It is fine to have the right answer – supposing you have – but the next problem is to convince others that it is the right answer. I would like you to give some thought to that before the next meeting. Come and have a chat with me after the meeting.'

Starting a New Job

A public servant is moved from one area of her department to another. She takes over an existing office, a diary of meetings and some statements of plans for the year. There is no discussion with her predecessor, because the decision to make a change was sudden and both of them had holidays which prevented them from meeting before her predecessor left for another part of the country.

On her first day she asked her Personal Assistant for some help. 'I need somebody to show me the system. I don't see any meeting arranged with my boss. Anyway I would like some briefings from someone else who has the broad picture. Who's been here longest and who might help me most? Is that two people or one?' 'It's really two people. Mr Robinson is the longest serving of your group, and he can be a bit sensitive so you might think it desirable to talk to him anyway. Mr Green was generally thought to be closest to your predecessor, and he has really been handling things for the month since Mr Thomas left.'

EXERCISE 3.1

1. Consider each of the cases above:

- Who was giving help to the main participants in each of them?
- How was the help given?
- How consciously was it provided as help?
- What kind of help do you believe it to have been?

EXERCISE 3.2

1. Have you had any experiences similar to those mentioned above?
2. Have you had other experiences different in form, but similar in their impact on you?

3.   Looking back, what do you think you learned from them?
4.   Who helped you – and in what way?

Commentary on the Exercises

Much of the help offered to individuals in learning from managerial work is initially directed solely at improved achievement of the managerial task. The helping aspect, if it is conscious and recognized at all, is similarly based on someone having been helped in carrying out a managerial task or resolving a problem. Learning from the experience is initially rarely analysed, articulated, and therefore conscious.

Cutting the Budget

This example of managerial work providing a learning experience is an example of an unplanned learning opportunity which became a consciously used opportunity. Help was provided by the boss, probably unconsciously, as a role model in how to carry out a particularly difficult task. More conscious help was provided by a colleague, through participation in a discussion on what the boss had done and what had been learned from it. Although they agreed on the main learning for them, each had made different observations.

Customer Care

In this case the hotel manager deliberately took his relatively new deputy along with him to see what the problem was. Equally deliberately he asked him afterwards how he would have handled it. This is a characteristic way in which someone finds out about one of the competences of a relatively new subordinate. In this case, several factors are involved in learning for the subordinate.

He has observed the boss at work. He has the chance to try out any ideas or questions he may have about how it could have been handled differently. He has the opportunity to generalize from the particular experience of handling a difficult customer. In addition, there are some important learning points for him on his relationship with his boss. How does he express any views he may have about how he might have handled the situation, without perhaps seeming critical of his boss?

Interestingly, in this case, the boss saw it as a mixture of issues. 'I thought it was a particularly difficult discussion, so I was genuinely interested in whether I might have handled it better. But even more I was interested in what he had seen and how he set about commenting to me. I thought he might have learned something about the problem and something about me – and now I expected to learn something about him.

'Mainly I saw it as observing how he would tackle things and what he had learned from the situation. I suppose I was helping him to learn by providing an opportunity to review.'

Project Z

Here the director had chosen his project group largely from people he knew and who he thought would make a good contribution in different ways to carrying out the task. The young Finance representative was chosen for that reason, with the supplementary point that he was regarded as a high flyer – not all the others on the group were similarly regarded. In his previous job the director had always been slightly cynical about some of the newer approaches to management development, and had never been very comfortable with the formal once a year appraisal of performance and development needs. In this case, his concern over the style of contribution of the Finance man was driven primarily by a feeling that some very useful ideas that needed to be properly understood by other participants in the group were being lost because of the unnecessarily aggressive know-it-all style of a relatively young manager. So the director's prime concern was with the performance of the group in the longer term.

Although the prime concern was with task, it also struck him that the young man might never have been given any guidance on how to influence other people. 'I thought here was a very bright guy with lots of potential to contribute, but so far he had only shown he was bright in the technical or professional sense. I thought I would give him the chance, first of all, to work out for himself what I meant about the need to influence others, and then see whether he could work out what he needed to do differently. I thought he was worth investing a bit of extra time and trouble on. I knew the last thing I should do, as someone 35 years older than him, was simply to sit him down and tell him that he needed to behave differently and to do it in the following ways.'

In this example, the director was really acting as a mentor. He was acting in the role of a wiser, more experienced person offering an observation on the manager's performance, not directly coaching him. Essentially the young man was being given the chance to learn through a more indirect approach which might work more effectively given the differences between the director and the manager. It is interesting to see that no direct coaching was involved – a process which probably would have horrified both of them if regarded as that. Note also that the mentor had refrained from any action which could have been misinterpreted by the manager's boss as interfering in his responsibility for developing the young manager.

Starting a New Job

This is a particularly interesting case because it deals with what can be the most stretching situation many managers encounter, moving into a new job with insufficient preparation or induction. Here, not only was there no help available from her predecessor, but the boss seems to have made no preparation or arrangements to see him. The individual clearly has taken the first responsibility for learning herself by recognizing some of her immediate needs. She has also sought help from someone almost entirely absent from management development literature – her Personal Assistant or Secretary. While subordinates sometimes deserve a mention – in my own research one or two examples were found – the secretary rarely does. This is a foolish undervaluing of the help such a person can provide, not only of course at the introductory stage as shown here but often throughout a manager's career. Of course, you have to be open to help. I remember a secretary coming to me with some feedback she had received via her own communication channels on a difficult situation in which I was involved. She told me she would not have dreamt of telling me (that is, helping me to learn from it) if I had not previously shown myself interested in her, her work, her problems and what she thought about the work I was doing.

Key Events in Learning at Work

Research on how managers learn from work experience in the United States was carried out by McCall and his colleagues. From their interviews they established five key events which were most frequently quoted by the managers they interviewed:

- Participation in projects or task forces;
- Switching job from line to staff;
- Starting from scratch, e.g. setting up a completely new plant or function;
- Turn around jobs;
- A leap in a job to something broader or very different.

Managers learned the following from these events:

1. *Projects/Task Forces*
   How to handle ignorance (perhaps including their own), and getting cooperation without line authority.
2. *Line to Staff Switches*
   Learning the difference between the hands-on action orientated line roles and the more reflective, persuasive style necessary in staff jobs.
3. *Starting from Scratch*
   Learning what was important and how to organize for it. Learning how to survive and generating confidence from doing so.
4. *Turn Around*
   How to be both tough and persuasive. How to be instrumental in carrying things through.
5. *Leap in Scope*
   Examples of this were moves within the same function or area, but also could involve moves to a new function or area. The kind of learning achieved was managing by less direct involvement on all issues.

Interestingly, another major learning achievement was the need to develop subordinates because in bigger jobs there is a need for more delegation.

Perhaps one of the most obvious, yet important, statements made in the book is that managers recognized they learned because they had to in order to succeed.

It is fascinating to see that they found that 20 per cent of the key events in the careers of the executives involved in their study featured a specific person rather than an assignment. Of those people 90 per cent were organizational superiors. It was rare to learn from either subordinates or peer colleagues.

My own research in the UK drew many similar conclusions. In addition to the general findings about the significance of learning from different kinds of work experience, we also found that experiences could be of different value in their measure of importance to the individual. Like McCall and his colleagues we found that the most important experiences were centred on the job itself, particularly when it was new, when there were changes in it, or when there were additions to the job – what we call stretching the boundaries – as well as specific projects and task forces. Unlike McCall, however, we found and gave emphasis to some other aspects.

First, we found many more examples of individuals learning within the existing job. Secondly, while agreeing with the emphasis McCall gives to the need to provide opportunities for learning, we concluded that many existing personnel systems were good at providing opportunities, as indeed were line managers in a less obvious sense, but that organizations were very bad at helping people to learn from those opportunities. Thirdly, we give much more emphasis to the nature of the learning process involved, and how individuals can be helped to understand it.

The view that many opportunities to learn arise within the existing job is shown in the first two of the examples at the beginning of this chapter. Stretching the job is illustrated by Project Z – only starting a new job involves relatively adventurous new learning.

Ironically, both those opportunities presented to individuals through normal work assignments, and frequently those presented through a planned management development route, are in practice delivered with the same lack of concern to identify what the learning opportunities really are. In the first case, the manager presenting the opportunity to a subordinate will rarely have thought about it except in the vaguest terms – 'You'll pick up some new experience through it'. In the second case, so-called planned management development rarely goes much beyond the manager's own statement – 'it will be a good chance for you to work with some different people and see how they handle problems which will also be a bit new to you'. In neither case is the learning element within the managerial assignment identified in a way which is helpful to the individual. I describe this situation as being Big O – the so-called 'big opportunity' which is often just a large blank area in terms of learning. It can also be a big zero in the learning achieved. I contrast this with managed learning opportunities. The important point here is that the management of the learning opportunity rests primarily with the manager setting up the work assignment, and secondly with the individual involved. Of course, the management development adviser may also have a helpful role to play, in suggesting individuals for assignments, or in discussing with the manager and the assignee what actually might be learned from it. The visual presentation of the alternatives is shown in Figures 3.1 and 3.2.

In this and the preceding chapter it is shown that having an experience is not the same as learning effectively from it. Nor is providing a learning opportunity the same as enabling someone to learn effectively from it. The essential element here is the provision of a more detailed analysis of what is involved in a learning opportunity, and also help for the individuals in understanding how they might learn from the opportunity. This latter point needs to be broken down into a general statement about the complete sequence of learning stages involved (The Learning Cycle), and the issue of individual preferences which may influence the extent to which people will learn at different stages of the cycle (The Learning Styles). These issues are discussed more fully in Chapter 4.

Seeing Activities as Learning Opportunities

A main task in helping individuals to recognize and make use of real work activities more effectively for learning is to identify them as specifically as possible. Of course it would often be best if this were done in advance of a potential learning opportunity. However, as we have seen, managerial life inevitably involves lots of things which are not planned and which cannot be properly analysed, anticipated and prepared for in advance. In practical terms a great deal of learning is secured by looking back over an event which you did not know in advance would present a learning experience.

EXERCISE 3.1

1. List the five main managerial activities you undertook last week.
2. Which were purely solitary involving only yourself?
3. Which involved other people in your own organization?
4. Were there chances to discuss what happened after the event?
5. Were you helped by such a discussion?
6. In what way were you helped?
7. What did you learn?

EXERCISE 3.2

1. What are the five main managerial activities in which you will be involved next week?

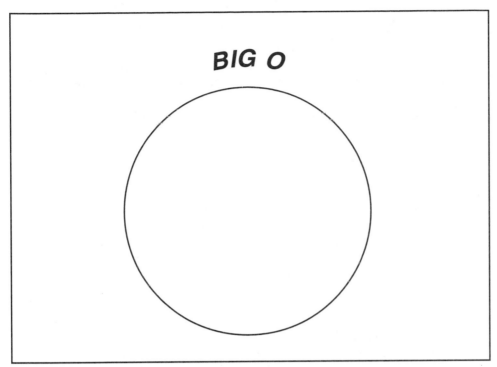

Figure 3.1   Big O

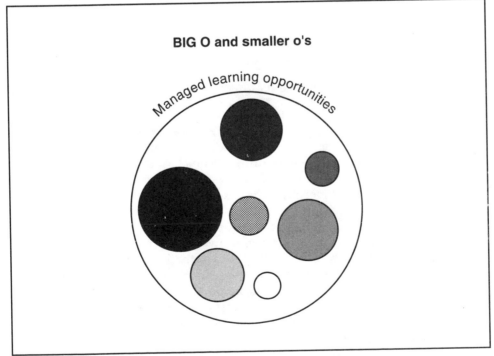

Figure 3.2   Big O and smaller o's

2.   Which of them involve other people?
3.   Is there anyone else involved who might help you identify in advance what is going to happen, and/or review with you afterwards what actually did happen?
4.   Can you identify now not only what might be happening in those five main activities, but what you might learn from them?

These exercises illustrate the application of the Retrospective and Prospective Approaches outlined in Chapter 2. The exercises require a manager to do the thinking, help being provided only by the stimulus of the general questions. Many managers may find this more of a struggle than they are willing to undertake. 'What do you mean by managerial activities?' 'How would you define main?' 'If I cannot remember clearly what the five main points were last week how on earth can I identify those that will come up next week!'

So it is helpful for many managers to provide a detailed list of possibilities. One way of doing this was developed by Peter Honey and myself (reprinted here with my co-author's permission). Managers should:

1.   Complete the exercise on their own learning
2.   Select a subordinate and complete it on their perception of the subordinate's use of Learning Opportunities

EXERCISE 3.3

For this exercise please see pages 39, 40 and 41.

Managing for Learning Results

Since we are describing a process which integrates management and learning it will probably be clear that there are some conceptual and practical difficulties in talking about measuring results. Most managers and their bosses will consider whether the activity has achieved something necessary to effective management. Indeed they are likely, even if influenced by a chapter such as this to consider the learning issues involved, subsequently to revert to considering the activity purely in terms of its management content rather than also as something involving or not involving achieved learning.

Primarily the need is to help them to continue to concentrate on both issues. As managers, they will review the effectiveness of a particular management activity as learners and helpers in learning; they should also review its achieved learning result. The process is essentially the same. In order to help managers understand the similarities between carrying out a task effectively, and learning effectively, I use Figure 3.3 (see p. 42).

When the two cycles are seen side by side managers quickly recognize the similarity between the two. Thinking about how they have carried out a task,

EXERCISE 3.3   FUTURE LEARNING OPPORTUNITIES

Here is a list of opportunities which may have been available to you, and from which you may have learned. First use Column 1 to indicate which you are already using.

Informal Opportunities	**Column 1** I am using this for learning now	**Column 2** I could use this in future
Stretching the job		
Boss		
Mentor		
Colleagues/Peers		
Subordinates		
Network contacts		
Projects		
Familiar tasks		
Unfamiliar tasks		
Task groups		
Problem solving with colleagues		
Domestic life		
Charitable work		
Professional groups		
Social committees		
Sporting clubs		
Reading		

Formal Opportunities

Formal Opportunities	Column 1 I am using this for learning now	Column 2 I could use this in future
Being coached		
Being counselled		
Having a mentor		
Job rotation		
Secondments		
Stretched boundaries		
Special projects		
Committees		
Task groups		
External activities		
Internal courses		
External courses		
Reading		

Summary of Column 1

Count up your ticks on Column 1 and position yourself on this scale:

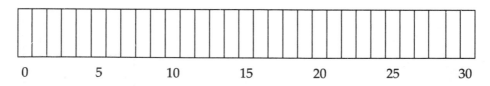

| 0 | 5 | 10 | 15 | 20 | 25 | 30 |

I am using a narrow
range of opportunities

I am using a wide range
of opportunities

In the light of your score on Column 1 items, can you now identify some extra opportunities which you could use in future? Use Column 2 to indicate future opportunities.

For each future opportunity you have identified in Column 2, consider what action you need to take to make it happen.

What I am going to do:

What action is required by someone else to get these future opportunities to occur?

What I need to get someone else to do:

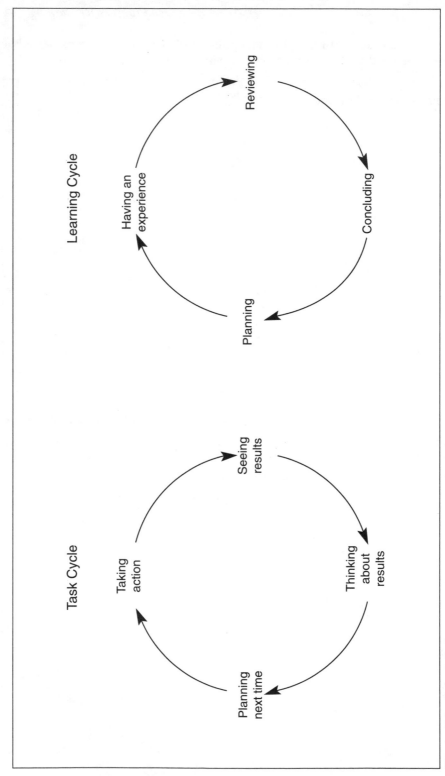

Figure 3.3 Separate Task and Learning Cycles

how successful it has been, what conclusions they draw from that success or failure, and what they will do next time is a familiar management process. Any managerial helper can therefore encourage the evaluation of success of a learning opportunity by the same process now described as the Learning Cycle. It is carrying through this cycle carefully and with appropriate balance which helps to convert Big O into achieved learning. It is the process which not only tells someone what has been learned but helps the very important stage of generalization – not just what I have learned by watching this particular difficult customer, but what I conclude from that for future encounters with difficult customers. Most importantly also it provides some of the motivation to undertake the more careful review of other learning opportunities – success breeds success.

Formal and Informal Types of Learning

Figure 3.4 presents my model of management development.

I have argued that we needed to embrace more fully, clearly and with greater time and commitment what I have called 'integrated managerial-opportunistic processes'. This chapter shows how some of the informal managerial-accidental processes work. Once they are reviewed and under-stood by the managers directly involved in them they can become integrated managerial-opportunistic processes. Of course the movement towards them can come from the slightly different direction of being encouraged through the formal management development system. An example would be setting up a project or task group. In the case presented above – Project Z – the construction of the task group, the position of the leading director, the participation of the individuals on the project were almost entirely manage-ment decisions made with a view to the task objectives and not to any learning objective. With the intervention, guidance and help of a manage-ment development or human resources specialist, of course, they might have been recognized and used earlier as learning opportunities. This kind of intervention is described in Chapters 9 and 10 where we discuss management development as a special process.

Type 1 Informal managerial-accidental processes

Characteristics   Occur with managerial activities
Explicit intention is task performance
No clear development objectives
Unstructured in development terms
Not planned in advance
Owned by managers

Development   Learning is real, direct, unconscious, insufficient
consequences

Type 2 Integrated managerial-opportunistic processes

Characteristics   Occur within managerial activities
Explicit intention both task performance and
   development
Clear development objectives
Structured for development by boss and subordinate
Planned beforehand or reviewed subsequently as
   learning experiences
Owned by managers

Development   Learning is real, direct, conscious, more substantial
consequences

Type 3 Formal management development-planned processes

Characteristics   Often away from normal managerial activities
Explicit intention is development
Clear development objectives
Structured for development by developers
Planned beforehand and reviewed subsequently as
   learning experiences
Owned more by developers than managers

Development   Learning may be real (through a job) or detached
consequences   (through a course)
is more likely to be conscious, relatively infrequent

Figure 3.4   Model of types of management development

4

The learning process

So far this book has primarily covered the situations from which managers could learn. When managers say they learn from experience, they generally mean the situations, not the process. Our first attempt to convey *how* managers learn was made through the 'Four Approaches' analysis, showing how managers engage in learning from experience. Now we turn to a more extensive discussion of how managers learn, both through work and courses.

Defining Words

Differences in the terminology used to describe the process of acquiring skills, knowledge, insight or changed attitudes provide material for academic debate. They seem rather less relevant to a busy line manager whose concern is often expressed simply as 'a wish to help people do better'. From a managerial point of view there are some distinctions which it is helpful to make because they will help managers see things in terms familiar and acceptable to them rather than to academic writers. A simple, understandable and reasonably accurate differentiation between the four main words is shown in Chart 4.1.

Chart 4.1 Words mean what I say they mean

Education	Knowledge provided through an institution part of the academic network.
Training	Skills provided through institutions, organisations or individuals not part of the academic network.
Learning	Knowledge, skills or insights obtained as a result of a planned or unplanned experience, of relatively immediate application.
Development	Improved understanding or insight obtained through a variety of life experiences, and applying to a broad view of personal growth.

I have offered these definitions with no great confidence that they would be widely accepted, but in order to make a point. An immediate disagreement would occur, for example, on the distinction between education and training. Many educational institutions actually carry out training processes, i.e. they deal in the development of skills – thus we have an apparently hybrid process called vocational training carried out in education institutions. Similarly the distinction between learning being concerned with issues of relatively immediate relevance and development being concerned with longer term issues of personal growth and satisfaction is one about which there would be argument. It is precisely because there is disagreement, lack of clarity and argument about these four terms that I have offered a definition which enables me to make my next point more effectively. When the distinctions in both principle and practice are so blurred, it seems of little relevance to ask managers to engage in discussion about the differences.

In fact it is more helpful for managers to concentrate on what is being delivered. As managers they are concerned essentially with outputs – what is achieved. Instead of engaging in the equivalent of the medieval disputation about how many angels can dance on the end of a pin, it is much more relevant for managers to think in terms of the difference between inputs and outputs. From this perspective, which is vital for the purposes of this chapter, there is one significant difference between these four words:

Education and training are both statements about inputs.
Learning and development are both statements about outputs.

While, no doubt, even this distinction could be questioned, it does, like the prospect of hanging, help concentrate the mind of a manager. There has been far too much attention paid to inputs, i.e. what is delivered to an individual, compared with outputs, i.e. what the individual actually knows or is able to do as a result of the inputs. All too many formal management development processes, whether the total system or elements in it such as Appraisal or courses, fit Oscar Wilde's comment on the reception of one of his plays – 'The play was a great success, but the audience a terrible failure'. One of the most useful questions a line manager can ask a personnel director, management development adviser, trainer or business school tutor is to describe not the sophistication of the techniques they are using to make inputs – 'we visited thirty companies before producing this revised Appraisal scheme' – but the consequences of what they are providing for the manager learner.

The Best News about Management Learning

The emphasis in this book so far has been on how individuals can learn through help provided around work experiences. The reasons given for this

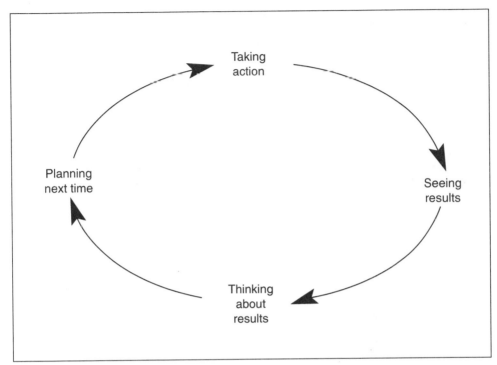

Figure 4.1   The Task Cycle

have been that these situations are so prevalent, and yet so under-utilized, that they provide the best, and indeed often cheapest, methods of securing productivity in learning. We can now add a different kind of statement about the association between carrying out managerial tasks and learning. As already indicated in Chapter 3, if you ask managers to describe the sequence of activities they go through in carrying out their managerial work, there is a high level of agreement. First they plan, then they carry out the task broadly according to the plan and they consider the results secured from whatever it is that they did. They then make up their mind about the success of failure, or partial success or failure, of their endeavour. Finally they decide what they will do if faced with the same problem or engaged in the same activity, or attempting to meet the same kind of opportunity. Of course managers are not always able to plan ahead of every managerial activity, so they quite often find themselves engaged in activities which they had not planned before-hand. A simplified model of this sequence of events is shown above in Figure 4.1 as 'The Task Cycle'.

If you take managers through a similar exercise of asking them to describe the process they go through when they learn, you will less frequently find them capable of delivering a neat sequence. This is not because learning is inherently more complicated, merely an indication of the fact that few managers have ever been asked to think about how they learn.

What we find in analysing the way in which people learn is that they go through a sequence based essentially on having some kind of experience. They do a piece of work or they engage in a task such as attending a meeting, visiting a customer, making a presentation or interviewing a candidate for a job. After the activity they think about what was involved in it, and whether the activity was successful or not – they reflect on the experience they have had. The third stage of their learning process is that they then draw some conclusions about the experience and their reflections on it. The conclusions may be related only to that particular experience, or they may draw together a number of similar experiences to construct a model, system or theory (though this latter is a word managers are often reluctant to use). Finally, from these three stages managers decide what to do, as a result of the collected processes undergone as part of this total learning sequence: having had an experience, looked seriously at it and drawn conclusions from it they then decide what to do next time. A simple, generalized example would be related to an interviewing experience:

'I carried out an interview with someone who worked for one of our competitors.

After the interview I sat down and looked over the notes I had made on the interview and what I had learned from the interviewee.

As a result of reading my notes I decided that I had become so interested in some of the different techniques and practices employed by our competitor that I had failed to draw out sufficiently what this particular interviewee had contributed to the success, as he claimed it, of his unit. I concluded that I ought to be more careful in future to be sure that I met the two different objectives of learning about the individual and his organization.

I drew up a plan for my next interview, which set out the questions I would ask under two different headings – information about the organization, and information about the individual.'

If we now put that sequence of events into a cycle we obtain a picture as shown in Figure 4.2 – 'The Learning Cycle'.

The good news about managerial learning is shown if we put the two cycles side by side (Figure 4.3). As will be evident the two cycles are remarkably similar. Both contain four stages, both represent the same kind of sequence of events and both contain the same kind of verbs. The good news is that when we are asking managers to learn we are not asking them to engage in a totally different kind of thinking process. Education and training have been very much concerned with trying to identify a thinking and working process which is distinguishably different from that in which managers normally think and behave. This is a gross and unnecessary error. Individuals do not have to transform themselves in order to be learners, from one thinking mode into another. They may be asked to give different emphasis to different kinds or stages in the learning process, but they do not have to transform themselves totally from a managerial thinking mode into a managerial learning mode. Thus the first proposition in this book, about learning from normal managerial work, has the twinned supports of practical availability and process compatibility.

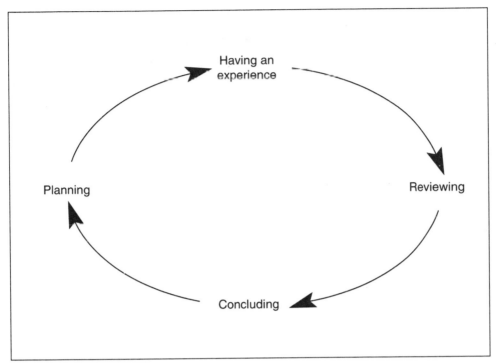

Figure 4.2   The Learning Cycle

Examples of the Learning Cycle in Operation

Chapter 3 included an example of a hotel manager offering his deputy a chance to learn, through an informal process, possibly unrecognized by either party. The boss was in effect offering to his subordinate:

- the chance to observe an attempt to placate a customer (the experience);
- the chance to consider what happened between the hotel manager and the customer (reviewing the experience); and
- the opportunity to decide what he, the deputy, might have done (draw conclusions from the experience).

To be complete as a Learning Cycle the manager would need to follow up whatever observations were offered by his deputy with a question such as 'So what would you do next time if you had to interview someone with a similar complaint?', which would be the 'planning the next step' stage.

Another example is taken from a visit by a group of managers to an organization offering the same services as their own organization, but in a different country. The visit involved:

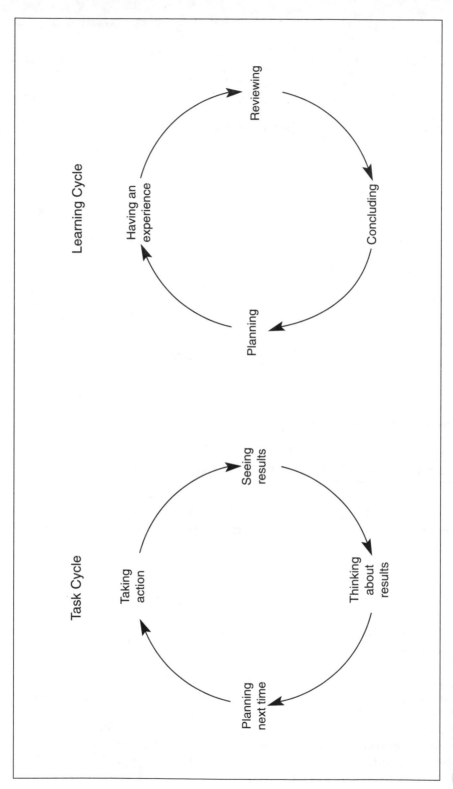

Figure 4.3 Task and Learning Cycles

- listening to presentations and walking the floor (the experience);
- sitting down in a group to discuss what had been seen and heard (reviewing);
- agreeing as a group on further questions drawn from conclusions arrived at through the discussion (concluding); and
- drawing up a plan of suggested actions for their organization back in their own country (planning the next step).

The contribution of the boss to the learning involved in this situation was that the visit was set up as a result of her initiative, and the final stage – presentation of conclusions and planning the next steps – were delivered to her by the group of managers involved in the visit. She thus provided an opportunity for a learning review.

Using the Learning Cycle

If all four stages of the Learning Cycle were properly followed, and if each stage was given appropriate emphasis, then several learning products would emerge. First, awareness of the Learning Cycle would enhance the likelihood that the full depth and range of possibilities within any learning opportunity were understood and implemented. Second, awareness of the four main stages would also identify one of the weaknesses in using learning opportunities effectively. Review and reflection is the stage which is most often given least serious attention. All too often managers leap from an experience to a decision about what to do next time without giving sufficient attention to analysing what has actually happened. One of the reasons why apparent successes are often inappropriately used later, thereby producing subsequent failures, is that insufficient critical reflection has occurred. In the pressure, excitement and stress involved in many managerial activities, the stimulus for action is greater than the motivation and rewards connected with calm and deliberate thought. Many managers seem to be implicit believers in Hamlet's comment:

> '. . . thus the native hue of resolution
> Is sicklied o'er with the pale cast of thought'.

However, we now have to challenge the two generalizations offered so far – that there is a desirable Learning Cycle which we should all go through in relation to every learning opportunity, and that managers in general are insufficiently geared to review and reflection. In fact we turn to the discovery about learning which is potentially exciting and enabling, though often initially encountered as difficult and problematic. It is the discovery or rediscovery that we are talking about individuals, not about the generalization, 'all managers'.

One Person's Meat . . .

The principle of the Learning Cycle, the view that any learning opportunity will be enhanced if serious attention is paid to all four stages, is valid. It is as true in relation to on-the-job experiences as it ought to be, but rarely is, in the design of off-the-job experiences. In the latter case course designers are gradually realizing that any programme which emphasizes wholly one stage at the expense of the others leads to unsatisfactory learning experiences for most participants. However, the general principle is made more difficult to apply by the fact that individuals vary considerably in their interest and capacity to learn from one stage of the cycle as compared with another. This can be seen as a fact of life to be coped with, an unfortunate aberration, or as an exciting demonstration of the infinite variability of individuals. Whatever your view, the practical effect is that recognition and use of the facts of individual differences in terms of preferred ways of learning is essential in providing effective help.

One way of illustrating the facts of individual differences that works across a number of different countries is the question of how people learned to play the most managerial of all games, golf. When this question is put to groups of managers their responses fall under the following four broad categories:

1. I picked up a second-hand set of golf clubs and a dozen golf balls and I went out to a nearby field and started to whack the ball into the distance. Putting was easier, I did that on the lawn at home.
2. I found a friend of mine who was a pretty good golfer; he operated at 10 handicap. I invited myself to go round with him several times just watching what he did and what his partners in a foursome did. I could actually see sometimes why he hit the ball straight and the others didn't.
3. I went out and bought some books and video tapes – Jack Nicklaus and Nick Faldo – read the books, studied the video and worked things over in my mind. I learned answers to questions like 'why your legs are more important than your arms when you are driving', and what terms like 'slice' and 'hook' really mean.
4. I decided that the best thing was to have lessons from a professional. I thought if he was good he would not only suggest the right techniques to me, but actually help me concentrate on the things that I could do rather than leaving me to try to do things that were really impossible for a beginner.

Of course not everyone plays golf. So try the following exercise.

EXERCISE 4.1

1. Think of a sporting or domestic activity, such as cooking or gardening. Can you identify four ways of learning, similar to those given in the golf example?

2. Do you believe that you would have a preference for one of these four?
3. Think of a managerial technique, skill or knowledge item which you have needed to acquire over the last two years. Have you been exposed to different ways of learning it? Have you found that you preferred one way to another?

The preferences individuals have for ways of learning are called Learning Styles.

So far in this analysis we have established only a general principle, that individuals differ. That statement has been tested against the experience of individual readers. However, if we remained at the level of generalization that people differ one from another, the cause of learning will not have advanced very far. In fact we will only have gone through two stages of the Learning Cycle:

- having an experience (reading a statement that individuals differ)
- reviewing the experience (does the statement work out if I apply it to myself?).

To complete the Learning Cycle, i.e. to generate the most effective learning from this particular section, readers need to draw some conclusions from the first two stages and then plan what to do as a result of those conclusions. One conclusion especially relevant for this book is that it would be helpful to identify the differences because then we could plan to do something about them with individuals.

Identifying Learning Styles

When we began our work on Learning Styles in the late 1970s, my colleague, Peter Honey, and I concluded (after reviewing our experiences) that learning was a manifestation of managerial and professional behaviour. We took the view that since managers learned most of what they learned through their managerial work, the best way of approaching their learning behaviour was through their managerial behaviour. So the Honey and Mumford Learning Styles Questionnaire, now used in many countries, which is based on descriptions of four significantly different Learning Styles, was devised. In summary, the four styles are:

Activists
- try anything once
- tend to revel in short-term crises, firefighting
- tend to thrive on the challenge of new experiences
- are relatively bored with implementation and longer-term consolidation
- constantly involve themselves with other people.

Reflectors	• like to stand back and review experiences from different perspectives
	• collect data and analyse it before coming to conclusions
	• like to consider all possible angles and implications before making a move
	• tend to be cautious
	• enjoy observing other people in action
	• often take a back seat in meetings.
Theorists	• are keen on assumptions, principles, theories, models and systems thinking
	• prize rationality and logic
	• tend to be detached and analytical
	• are unhappy with subjective or ambiguous experiences
	• are tidy and fit tasks into rational schemes.
Pragmatists	• search out new ideas or techniques which might apply in their situation
	• take the first opportunity to experiment with applications
	• respond to problems and opportunities 'as a challenge'
	• are keen to use relevant ideas from management courses
	• like to get on with things with clear purpose.

The styles replicate the four stages of the Learning Cycle as shown in Figure 4.4.

The statistical analysis we have carried out on the results from over 4000 managers and professional people shows that only 20 per cent of them emerge with three strong preferences, i.e. could be seen as potentially good all round learners. In contrast, 35 per cent of managers had one strong preference. Whether you look at the results concentrating on strong preferences, that is those learning activities to which a person will tend to respond positively, or look at the low scores which suggest that an individual will tend to respond less well to activities defined by that style, the implications for the individual learner and therefore for the helper of the individual learner are dramatic. While the principle of balanced progress in the Learning Cycle must be sustained, the preferences of individuals within that cycle can now be recognized and catered for. At the macro level, for example, if an individual is to be seconded to another activity or involved in a project we must not only ensure that each stage of the cycle is addressed through the project or secondment, but we must respond to the reaction of individuals to each stage of the cycle. The Activist, who quite enjoys being thrown in at the deep end, will not be too concerned if placed suddenly into a project or task group with very little warning or opportunity to think about what is involved. The more cautious Reflector will want to know about issues such as terms of reference, time scale, and so on. Whereas the former may well participate fully and enjoy the experience, the danger is that opportunities for learning are insufficiently identified through a failure to review. The strong Reflector, in contrast, may be unduly cautious and operate at too low

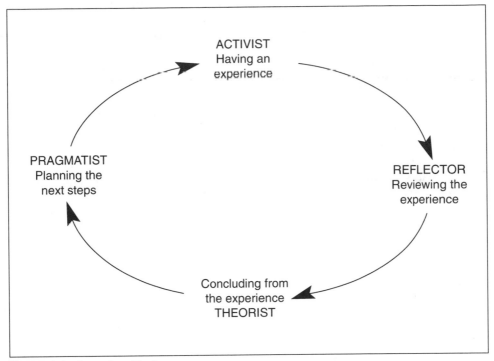

Figure 4.4   Learning Cycle

key a level to acquire all the experiences which might be available through a project or secondment.

Similar issues arise in relation to the expression of preferences when individuals are exposed to formal training or education. Here is an extract from a course brochure:

'The emphasis throughout the programme is on the integration of the various aspects of marketing into a coherent strategy, the coordination of marketing with other functions of the company, and the development of a symbiotic relationship between the company and its environment.'

A course of this kind emphasizing strategy, coordination and the development of a symbiotic relationship will be attractive to Theorists, certainly in language and probably also in delivery. At the other end of the scale someone with a low Theorist score would probably be repelled both by language and the actuality. Another example, in quite a different mode, is a course using outdoor activities. If properly designed such courses can offer something to suit all four of the styles, but unfortunately there are still a good many which emphasize the physical exercises to the extent that they are only suitable for Activists. The answer for the individual is to look at the detail of the programme and preferably arrange to have some debriefing from previous participants to ensure that there is provision for significant opportunities to reflect on the physical activities undertaken, and to construct and develop models of leadership from the experiences on the course.

Validating and Using Learning Styles

As with any questionnaire, an important issue is not only whether the LSQ produces a score, but whether that score is reliable and valid in a technical sense. The 'technical issues are covered in the material referred to in Further Reading (page 211). A valid and reliable view of the Learning Style preferences of any individual can only be secured by working through the full questionnaire. However, as an interim step, but only as a provisional introduction to the concepts, it can be helpful to undertake the following exercises.

EXERCISE 4.2

1. Look at the four summaries of Learning Styles on pages 53–4.
2. Score yourself on a scale of 0 to 10 where 0 = nothing like me, 10 = very like me.
3. Do you find that you have a high score on one style, and a low score on others?

Note 1
The scores are independent for each style – it is quite possible to have more than one high score.

Note 2
This exercise is valuable only as an introduction to the more serious and valid exercise of completing the Learning Styles Questionnaire. It does, however, enable readers to tackle the next exercise as a way of introducing another major aspect of how Learning Styles influence effective help.

EXERCISE 4.3

1. Identify an individual whose development you are currently trying to assist.
2. Score that individual on the scale of 0 = nothing like, 10 = very like.
3. Compare any high or low scores with those you have established for yourself.
4. Are there significant differences in the prediction based on this initial exercise of how that individual may prefer to learn as compared with how you prefer to learn?
5. What information or data do you have on how that individual has responded to different kinds of learning opportunity, which may confirm or challenge this view?

EXERCISE 4.4

1. Return to the learning golf example on page 52. Can you identify the four Learning Styles in operation?
2. Look at your answers to Exercise 4.1. Do your responses match the four Learning Styles and your own preferences?
3. See page 64 for the answer to (1) above.

If it were possible to identify Learning Styles on the basis of a quick review of four short descriptions, then it would not be necessary to produce a reliable and valid 80-item questionnaire. The exercises that the reader may just have completed have been provided in order to sustain the flow of argument in the book. Experience also shows that they provide enough information and intrigue managers sufficiently for them to want to follow through with the required next step, which is to do the LSQ themselves, and to ask any individuals, to whom they are offering help, to complete the LSQ as well. Full technical guidance on this is provided in our *Manual of Learning Styles*.

The results of the LSQ can be used in every kind of learning situation:

- A boss and subordinate can generate greater mutual understanding of how each is likely to approach a learning opportunity. For example, Activist bosses and Reflector subordinates are helped to negotiate a better path than that otherwise available from mutual incomprehension.
- Mentors and learners similarly can work out some very important aspects of their relationship. Does the Pragmatist learner really only want to be provided with opportunities directly related to the immediate job, whereas the Theorist mentor wants to provide a wide range of opportunities of little immediate relevance to the learner?
- If an individual has one strong learning preference and is being nominated for a particular course, how congruent is that preference with the way in which the course will be run?
- If the management group wants to conduct a short learning review at the end of each management meeting, how do you encourage Activists not to rush out saying that they have important things to do? How do you employ the potential of the strong Reflector?

These questions and many others are covered in more detail in Chapters 7 and 8. Those chapters also address the issue of how to develop a wider range of Learning Styles in individuals, so that they are better equipped to be all-round learners from a variety of learning opportunities.

Encouraging Reflection

Even those individuals whose Learning Style provides the potential for learning from reflection are not always equipped with the means of doing so.

It was suggested earlier in this chapter that there is a general problem of encouraging managers to be sufficiently reflective, in the energetic turbulence of many managerial lives. For those who have a strong Reflector preference, the solution is relatively straightforward. They will be more than happy to take up the idea of a Learning Log or Management Diary. Activists are at the other extreme – they are usually very unwilling to devote serious thought and attention through written reflection. Paradoxically, of course, they are precisely the people who therefore need most encouragement to do so! In the course context, various disciplines can be encouraged or insisted upon which require people to keep a Learning Log. In working life it is more difficult to insist on such processes, but it can and should be done, certainly in relation to any formal management development process. Any individual who is supposed to be learning through a formal structured activity ought to be asked to keep a Log and to review the entries with an appropriate person – a training adviser sometimes, but preferably a boss, mentor or colleague.

In day-to-day management it is impossible to insist on an individual keeping a Learning Log. An Activist boss and an Activist subordinate are most unlikely to want to do so! A Reflector boss and Activist subordinate can negotiate a helpful arrangement here. The Reflector boss can suggest that they have a regular meeting to review what the subordinate has been involved in and what has been learned. Without insisting on a formal written document beforehand, the boss can at least ensure that notes are written up after discussion.

The two extremes have been identified above. Pragmatists often react well to the idea of a Learning Log because it enables them to pick out usable techniques, to experiment with them and then to decide how useful they have been. Strong Theorists can be influenced to keep a diary if the suggestion is made that it is directed very much at trying to produce links between experiences with the idea of testing out theories or models or even generating them.

Of course, the term Learning Log is not attractive to all managers, especially away from the formal context of management development. Charts 4.2–4 give various ways of using the same basic idea – generating more

Chart 4.2   The Filofax method

There are a variety of 'personal organizers' on the market which provide a convenient and flexible method of systematizing the various do-lists, checklists and planners that many managers use. So ways of improving learning can simply be to write some notes into your planner, as follows:

1. Make a note each day of the most interesting experience you have had. For example put a red ring round it in your planner or diary.
2. At the end of the day, or certainly at the end of each week, do a quick summary of the things you have learned from those most interesting experiences.
3. Transfer those learning experiences to a separate sheet, and write into your planner that you will review that sheet every three months.

Chart 4.3   The Management Diary

While many Filofaxes and planners provide a very small space to record activities, it is possible to make use of the more extensive space available in other forms of diary. A useful approach where you have more space is to undertake a weekly analysis using the following headings:

- What were the big problems in the week?
- What were the big opportunities?
- What new experiences did I encounter?
- What new look did I give to old experiences?
- So, what were the major things I learned this week?
- What new things might be coming up next week?

effective review of management experiences which are learning experiences as well. The helping manager could suggest any of these alternatives. It aids credibility if the helper can say from personal experience that one of the methods has been used by the helper.

Whereas Charts 4.2 and 4.3 have shown how to improve reflection on learning from normal work experiences, the Learning Log shown in Chart 4.4 is more explicitly geared to an even more careful identification of learning from structured learning experiences. The completion of a Learning Log should be seen as an essential component of the Learning Cycle. In comparison with our first two charts, which tend to focus particularly on establishing some reflection on experience, the properly designed Learning Log will take people through all three stages of the Learning Cycle after the experience. It will first enable an individual to capture and reflect on what has happened. Second, it provides an opportunity to relate that experience and reflection process to other experiences and other data, thereby taking an individual towards effective generalization. Finally it provides the opportunity to plan how to apply any learning that has been acquired.

The great difficulty about the Learning Log or Management Diary approach is that even where individuals can be encouraged to start them, they often lack the motivation and encouragement necessary to sustain the process. This is precisely where the managerial helper comes in. Boss, mentor and colleagues are all individuals who can provide the ideas suggested in this chapter, and then help an individual to sustain effort by discussing the results. Personal analysis and review is absolutely important, and it may well be that some aspects of that cannot be shared with other individuals – especially sometimes the boss! But a great deal can and should be shared, for two reasons. The first, as already suggested, is that this is a very effective way of sustaining the effort – the knowledge that you will be asked by boss, mentor or colleague what significant entries you have made this week is part of the discipline of sustaining the process. The second reason is that sharing generates additional knowledge or greater insight, through someone else's observation of the experience which you are discussing.

One of the themes of this book has been that manager developers will be best equipped to help others learn if they understand, and preferably

Chart 4.4　The Learning Log

Here is one way of keeping a Learning Log:

1. Decide in what physical form you want to keep it. Do you want a blank exercise book, a diary, or just to keep notes in some other form?
2. Write in your normal work diary some points which will remind you to keep the Learning Log! For example, write in every Friday 'Have I brought my Learning Log up-to-date?'.
3. Write down in whatever form you think appropriate, i.e. notes or sentences, the experiences you have had on any particular day (preferably) or during a complete week.
4. Write up the experience – what happened, what you felt about it, what seemed to you to be the contribution of other people – purely as a descriptive statement.
5. Write down what conclusions you have drawn from the experience or collection of experiences.
6. Note that it is only at this stage that you are really trying to register learning points – up to now you have only set about recording. This is a very important point: if you rush ahead from the experience to 'what I have learned' without adequate analysis and reflection, the learning will be insufficient and indeed may be inaccurate.
7. As a result of your conclusions decide what actions you will take in relation to the particular experiences. What are you going to do?
8. Think ahead. It may be that what you have discovered by reviewing a particular experience or collection of experiences would have been improved if you had, for example, kept some notes at the time rather than relying on your memory. So there might be process points for you for a future occasion. Secondly, you might decide to think about the experiences to come. What might happen at next week's important budget presentation? Which new manager are you going to see in action on a visit to a supplier?
9. Draw up an action plan for yourself which covers both the process by which you learn and the possible content. Remember that your action plan needs to include both what you are going to do and when you are going to do it.

Chart 4.5　Learning Log on helping others develop

1. Who have I been trying to help?
2. What kind of help have I been offering around job experiences?
3. What other kind of help have I offered?
4. What has been the response of the learner to my help?
5. What other indications do I have of whether the help has been useful to the learner?
6. Why has my help been accepted and useful – or otherwise?
7. What conclusions do I draw for future action with this individual?
8. What conclusions do I draw for future action with other people?
9. What conclusions do I draw about the way in which I like help to be offered to me?

improve, their own use of learning opportunities, procedures, skills and styles. It is obvious therefore that manager developers should themselves consider how using a Learning Log or any of the other versions mentioned here could assist their own learning. Less obvious, but especially important in the context of this book, is the idea that they could keep a Learning Log on the helping processes they have used with different individuals. Chart 4.5 indicates the kind of uses to be considered.

It will be noticed that, in relation to many of the opportunities covered in this book, the manager developer's Learning Log will be a review of a continuous, or at least frequent, series of helpful interventions in and around the job. It is the connectedness of help which makes a Log worthwhile in relation to a particular individual. A Log recording only responses to offers of courses is less worthwhile.

EXERCISE 4.5   USING A LEARNING LOG

1.   Think of individuals whom you are trying to help develop.
2.   Which of them are most likely to respond favourably to a suggestion they should keep a Log (remember Activists are least likely to accept)?
3.   What specific activity/opportunity in this managerial work could you use as the initial focus of the Log?

Other Influences on Learning

Of course, there are a number of other factors which affect whether an individual learns or not. These are shown in Figure 4.5 'Influences on learning' (see p. 62). This figure brings into play a wide variety of influences, some at the macro level – organization structure and culture – some at the individual level – learning skills, attitudes and emotions. While this figure has been included here in order to show that there is more to effective learning than the Learning Cycle and Learning Styles, detailed discussion of the issues identified in the figure is contained in the next chapter.

Learning as a Progressive Cycle

Once the principle of the Learning Cycle has been understood, it is possible to develop it into a more sophisticated model. One version is the Learning Spiral, which Honey and I explain in our *Manual of Learning Styles*. This indicates the idea of each learning activity leading into further learning built from that activity. For the purpose of this chapter, I offer the rather different idea of improving learning within the original activity. The original Learning Cycle may show that the learner needs to review a stage in the cycle, e.g. by collecting and reviewing data more carefully, or the learner may need to check whether the concluding stage has led to a sensible conclusion. (For example, do all red-haired people have bad tempers?) Figure 4.6 'The Progressive Learning Cycle' illustrates this.

Chapter 2 presented the idea that while all managers claim to learn from experience, the timing and nature of their learning varied according to the

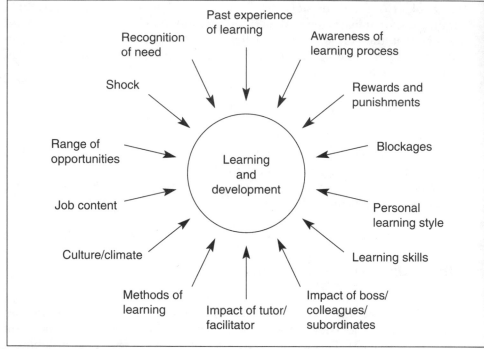

Figure 4.5   Influences on learning

Four Approaches – Intuitive, Incidental, Retrospective and Prospective. Clearly, this is a different way of looking at how managers learn. It was introduced in Chapter 2 because it focuses most directly on managerial experience as the prime cause of learning. As a model it is drawn from experiences at work, and is not yet proven as an explanation of the total learning process, applying equally to courses, as the Learning Cycle does. Nor do we yet have hard evidence, as we do with Learning Styles, that individuals have a dominating propensity to adopt consistently only one of the Four Approaches. Some manager developers will find the model helpful in suggesting to learners how they can improve the range and depth of their ability to learn from work experiences. Guidance on how this can be achieved is indicated in the material covered in Further Reading.

EXERCISE 4.6

1. Return to the details presented on the Four Approaches in Chapter 2.
2. Can you identify

   - a current managerial situation, or
   - a learner for whom you have responsibility

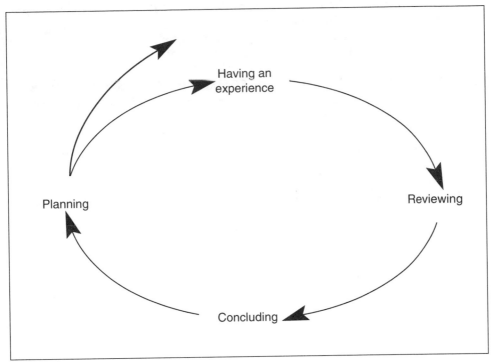

Figure 4.6 The Progressive Learning Cycle

where it might be helpful to use the Four Approaches model to improve learning?

Example

'We are very good at analysing dramatic failures and learning from them (Incidental Approach). We are not good at reviewing all the important things we do, to make sure we learn from them (Retrospective).'

'Jane is good at keeping a regular Learning Log, but she could benefit from moving from a purely Retrospective Approach to using the Prospective Approach – working out some things in advance.'

EXERCISE 4.7

1. Consider the experiences you have had in trying to help someone else develop; choose one or two individuals.

2. How far might the ideas given in this chapter have helped you to assist them even more than you did?
3. Which of the ideas would have been most helpful?
4. Which of the ideas might be most helpful with the individuals you have identified in Exercises 4.5 and 4.6 above?
5. Think of a recent management experience you have had, involving someone whose development you are trying to help. Does the Learning Cycle give you ideas on how to improve the kind of help you are offering?
6. Think of an individual you are trying to help. How might you use the Learning Styles Questionnaire to improve the help you are offering?

The Answers to Exercise 4.4

The methods described would be likely to suit, in the sequence given, the Activist, Reflector, Theorist, Pragmatist.

PART II
THE ART AND CRAFT
OF DEVELOPING MANAGERS

5

Ways of helping

Help is Defined by the Person Helped

One of the most important points for the manager developer is to accept at this point in the book a rather paradoxical proposition. So far, it has been shown how much more can be provided by managers in developing others. Yet the paradox is that help is defined not necessarily by an increase in the range, depth and quality of the help that is offered. In the same way that we have focused on output – learning – rather than input – training or education – so we also need to see help in terms of what is actually received not just as what is offered. We need to be concerned with results, not merely intentions. We know very well from many experiences of life that, for example, the help offered by parents to children can be seen as interference if it is offered in the wrong way at the wrong time, or on what the child sees as the wrong issue. The same situation can arise in management for the same reasons. The psychological factors are often enhanced with adults, who may be even less inclined to be put in a position of apparent subservience and dependence.

The proposals so far have been that the manager, as developer, can help others:

- recognize learning opportunities;
- understand what is involved in learning opportunities;
- use learning opportunities.

But the way in which help is offered at each of these stages will influence the extent to which the person being helped is willing to respond positively to the help being offered. It is important that managers think of the issues on which help can be provided and how it can be provided because otherwise they may enthusiastically offer help which is rejected. The consequence of this, naturally enough, is that the manager ceases to offer help either to the particular individual or, even worse, to others. So, of course, it is much better to avoid the possibility of rejection by giving at least some thought to what the person being helped might be willing to accept.

What Makes an Individual Interested?

The argument in this book has been that, in the main, individuals are interested in learning and development opportunities as ways of improving their personal performance. In some cases that concern or interest can be supplemented or concentrated on the improvement of the performance of the unit for which they are responsible. Primarily, the interest in help is created by some awareness of *need*. That awareness is in turn influenced by feelings about what an individual *wants* to improve. These needs and wants are revealed in a particular working situation – a problem, an opportunity or a relationship with an individual. The situation creates an opportunity, which needs to be recognized by both the manager helper and the individual as being appropriate. All these factors create the circumstances in which help might be appropriate and accepted. Help will only be received and used if the timing of the offer of help is appropriate, and if the way in which it is to be delivered is felt to be comfortable by the individual. Finally, surrounding all these aspects is the totality of the environment in which the individual is working – the organizational structure and, more importantly, the accepted modes of behaviour within the organization – its organizational culture.

All these can be seen as in various ways objective features of the situation. Their application is determined by the characteristics of the person for whom help might objectively be appropriate, but whose personal make-up will determine whether help is accepted. These aspects are summarized in Chart 5.1.

Chart 5.1   Why help is accepted

Objective needs
Felt wants
Managerial situation (demand, problems, opportunities)
Recognition of learning opportunity
Timing of offer of help
Style of help
Working environment (organization structure, style of management)
Personal characteristics of learner

Person to Person Help

For most individuals most of the time the kind of help to which they will respond will tend to relate to immediate issues of performance – what skills, what behaviour and what knowledge are needed to do this job well or better? Most managers will also want to offer help at this level because it is the level which they are most likely to understand. The nature of the help will often be in stating needs rather than in providing direct coaching. They are, for example, more likely to suggest that someone needs to be more assertive than to provide guidance on how to achieve this.

They are even less inclined to deal with underlying causes, especially those often categorized as 'personal', such as feelings of insecurity or inability to deal with stress. The reason for this approach is clear enough. Managers rarely have the time or inclination to go into deeper issues, both because it is the nature of managerial life to tend to deal with the immediate problem and also because many of them will feel a reluctance to become involved in some deeper issues. Understandably, and sometimes rightly, they see some of the larger scale and deeper issues about a manager's performance as being things which ought to be addressed through some specifically designed learning experience such as a course.

Two illustrations of the extremes will clarify the alternatives here.

John, Time and Help – Case 1

A supervisor is notorious for an inability to control the use of his time. His own meetings constantly overrun; he is late for meetings run even by very senior people in his organization. He fixes appointments which he does not keep. However, this weakness has been, though recognized, largely ignored in the past, because he is seen as 'brilliant' in nearly every other respect of his job. 'Say what you like about John, but if you look at the results in his department, his poor timing is something we have to put up with.'

A new manager arrives to take responsibility for John. After a month's experience he calls in John for a preliminary appraisal of his performance, and having identified John's positive achievements, raises the question of timekeeping. John agrees that he has a problem and that he would like to do something about it. The new manager suggests that John sets himself a modest target, for example, arriving punctually at four meetings in the week. He also suggests that he reads some material on managing time, and says that after a month of John trying to work to a new pattern they will discuss together whether a 'Managing Time' course might be helpful.

John, Time and Help – Case 2

The new manager in the case above himself attends a management course, and is asked to present a current problem which she would like to discuss with the other members of the course. She goes through the 'John' case outlined above. After some general discussion the tutor guiding the discussion asks a question. 'Have you thought that this kind of behaviour in someone who otherwise seems very efficient must have some deeper psychological cause? Almost certainly John has been through some other experience in which he has either been punished for being on time or rewarded for being late. Or perhaps he just wants to draw attention to himself. Isn't there a danger that in tackling the most obvious but surface demonstrations of John's behaviour you are failing to identify and therefore failing to tackle the real problem?'

These two cases illustrate both the general point about the level of intervention which helpers might be willing to offer, and also the level of intervention which an individual might be prepared to receive'. John was prepared to receive help with a matter he recognized as a problem, at a level which was recognizably managerial. We cannot be sure what his reaction would be if his new boss offered help along the lines indicated by the tutor, but we might well believe that, except within the protected confines of a management course, the kind of questions asked are not those most managers would put to potential learners in the real work situation. That is not to say they are bad or unhelpful questions – merely a comment about the kind of help that most managers will want to provide. Indeed in the second stage of the case quoted above, the new boss decided to consider the possibility of intervention not by herself but by someone with professional skills in that area.

EXERCISE 5.1   PERSON TO PERSON HELP

1.   Is it your experience that both as helper and as learner you have most often been offered help at the level of immediate or surface needs?
2.   Have you ever been offered help or given help yourself on deeper issues?
3.   What is your conclusion about the nature of the help you have been offered in the past?
4.   What is your conclusion about the nature of the help you have offered others up to now?

Person to Person Around the Job

We have seen many of the circumstances in which a person can be helped to develop in and around the work. Indeed the nature of the help offered and the reasons for offering it can be defined by what is initiating the help. While, as already indicated, the initial stimulus is likely to be immediate job performance, and therefore the help is aimed at improving managerial ability, the extent to which this is then supplemented by attention to the learning issues involved, or indeed even transformed into a learning opportunity, is of great importance. This is shown in Figure 5.1.

As we have seen so frequently in this book, concentration on performance creates the need, helps to identify the situation and provides motivation and commitment. As the attention is on performance requirements, to achieve results, insufficient attention may be given to what is actually happening in learning terms, or to delivering help in the way most acceptable to the learner. Equally, especially in structured learning situations, the emphasis on

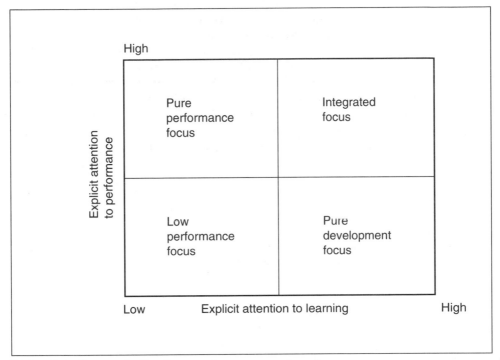

Figure 5.1   Focus of attention: performance or learning

learning may be such as to offer no real connection with management performance, or no clear association between the learning and relevant performance. This book argues for a better balance.

A specific illustration of relatively high or low emphasis on performance or learning can be seen in some of the problem solving examples used earlier in this book. Problem solving involves help directed at resolving particular problems or working on opportunities. Bosses, grand bosses, mentors, colleagues and subordinates may all offer help in this area. The problem solving approach starts with managerial concerns and imperatives, and then may become transformed in the formal management development context into an explicitly developmental approach called coaching, which has a strong emphasis on learning. This is an example of the general proposition visualized in Figure 5.1.

The problem solving/coaching approach is one which most managers have had offered to them, and which they use in offering help to others. It is the most directive form of help, and many include statements more often than questions. 'Why don't you . . .' 'When I had an experience like this what I did was . . .' 'Let me give you some feedback on how you made that presentation, and some suggestions on how to do it better.'

A less directive approach deals more in questions than in statements. It is an approach through which people are counselled rather than coached. In effect the counsellor is operating as a sounding board or listening ear – enabling an individual to describe circumstances, problems or opportunities primarily, or at least first in the discussion!

As we shall see in Chapter 7, the skills involved, the way in which help is offered, do not vary substantially between informal and formal processes. They can be highlighted in the formal process of coaching, as compared with the informal process of problem solving, simply as a means of giving greater urgency and priority to the effort involved.

One need for the potential helper therefore is to try and adopt the helping style best related to specific problems and opportunities, varied by the probable response of an individual to that situation and to a particular style of help:

- Who wants a general discussion of the problem with lots of input but no decisions by the helper?
- Who wants to be given direct indications of what to do and how to do it?
- Who wants simply an opportunity to talk through some aspect of managerial life?

Finally in this section we need to turn again to Figure 5.1. Whatever the managerial circumstance, the preferred styles of manager and learner, the approach suggested through this book is that the helper concentrates on learning opportunities within certain managerial situations. The greatest learning and development achievements will result from improved recognition and use of learning opportunities.

EXERCISE 5.2   THE FOCUS OF ATTENTION

1. Consider at least one recent case which you now recognize as an opportunity to help someone else learn.
2. Place the kind of help you offered within Chart 5.1 – was it high on attention to performance, and high also on attention to learning?
3. Was it low on attention to performance but high on attention to learning?
4. Was it high on attention to performance but low on attention to learning?
5. If you were faced with a similar situation, how might you adjust the attention to create a more balanced approach?

Person to Person – The Longer Term

The emphasis so far has been on needs arising in relation to performance within the current job. Of course many people want, and sometimes receive, help in planning future jobs. As Chapter 9 shows, this is often one of the prime purposes of formal management development through the systems of Appraisal, Potential Identification and Succession Planning. Sometimes, of course, the formal system specifies that an individual can progress no further. Although that may not be immediately experienced as the most useful of statements, subsequent reflection may show that that was precisely the most helpful thing to say.

Whatever the provisions of the formal system, informal networks, contacts and discussions all provide guidance on the future as well. Sometimes, confusingly, a boss will tell an individual two different things, one within the formal system, one outside it. Within the formal system he may give carefully planned feedback to encourage an individual to stay with the organization. Outside it, perhaps even outside the office, the advice may be different: 'I would not stay if I were you'. Indeed there can be considerable conflict in the mind of some managers when faced with the question of exactly what advice they should offer. Clearly it is expected that a manager will offer the advice which is most helpful to the organization – which may not necessarily be advice most helpful to the individual. 'If I were honest I would tell her that she stands no chance of promotion. Our formal policy talks about equal opportunities, but I know from other cases that something would always be found to prevent a woman being promoted. The organization expects me to tell her how equality is ensured – and it does not expect me to tell her that the informal arrangements will always beat the formal system.'

There may be considerable tension in the responsibilities of the boss. This is, of course, an area where mentors, to some degree, and colleagues, almost entirely, can offer more helpful advice. They do not carry the same authority – but equally they have less need to bend to organizational requirements.

In planning an individual's career, future possibilities need to be explored. A range of possibilities needs to be considered in formal career planning, as indicated in Chart 5.2.

Chart 5.2 Person to person – Planning the future

Stay in this job

Similar level job elsewhere in the organization

Different job, same level, same organization

Same job in another organization

Different job, same level in another organization

Promotion, this organization

Promotion to another organization

Substantially different job/career.

Individual Learning Preferences

This chapter started with the general proposition that what is seen as help by the learner is not necessarily the same as that offered by the helper. One of the most important aspects of this, of course, is the way in which any help is delivered (see Chapter 6), and specifically the question of whether the style and content of the help is congruent with the learning styles of the individual being helped. As Chapter 4 showed, the kind of help that an unaware Activist may offer a Reflector will create dissonance, dissatisfaction and deterence – the three Ds, leading to a fourth D – disaster.

Some More Different Than Others

The person who is in a position to be helped may be different from the helper in many respects, some of which we have already touched on and others which are covered in the next chapter. Some of the most significant issues may arise if there are differences of sex, ethnic origin or personal physical circumstances. The point is that while all helping relationships have to be based on the primacy of the individual being helped, learners in minority categories such as these have to be recognized as requiring special attention. Of course, that statement itself would not be accepted by everybody. While there are many male managers who hide the reality of their prejudices behind superficial declarations in favour of equality, there are also female managers who want their female juniors to go through the same torture and obstructed processes that they probably went through. 'I believe in promotion by merit, not by tokenism or so-called positive discrimination.'

The fact is that all three of these groups are disadvantaged in many ways. Many of them will therefore need different kinds of help. It is also the case that they need that help to be tendered in a way which recognizes those disadvantages, and yet manages not to patronize them. In other words, this is an area of great difficulty!

Managers facing these problems should find some way of testing their likely espousal of theories of equality and non-discrimination. There are profound difficulties for many managers in coping with relationships of this kind, difficulties so productive of tension and guilt that it is all too easy for a manager to proclaim 'I couldn't care less what someone's sex is or what the colour of their skin is'. The beliefs of many male, white, middle-class, able-bodied managers unfortunately do not correspond with the actual experience of the three groups identified in this section.

It will be noted that this section has been written mainly from the perspective that the helper is, like the majority of British managers, male and white. The stated problem has been so far with a learner not with these characteristics. Of course, there are issues arising the other way round – where the manager is female or of a different racial origin from the learner.

While this situation must not be ignored, at the moment it is the former case that is the more likely.

EXERCISE 5.3

1. Do you have people working for you who fit into one or more of the groups identified above?
2. Have you had problems in dealing with their learning needs, which you attribute to these particular kinds of difference?
3. Have you felt able to discuss the issues with the individual concerned?
4. Have you felt able to discuss the issues with someone else who might help you and the other person tackle the problems more successfully?

Personal Barriers to being Helped

Figure 4.5, Influences on learning (see page 62), identifies a number of factors, many of them related to the personal characteristics of the individual. Attitudes and emotions form part of the area of potential blockages to learning. Peter Honey and I have developed a questionnaire which helps to identify the extent to which people are released or inhibited by their attitudes and emotions (see Further Reading). Some examples of our questions are:

*   When things are going well I tend to leave them alone;
    or
    When things are going well I look for ways to get them to go even better.
*   I find it easy to be spontaneous;
    or
    I find it difficult to be spontaneous.
*   When someone criticizes me I feel curious;
    or
    When someone criticizes me I feel defensive and/or annoyed.

These are three samples of paired questions (in which you respond to one or other in the pair) which can help to indicate a possible response of a person to learning situations, and, as will be seen, to offers of help. The question on criticism is a particularly relevant one. Many managers think they provide 'helpful feedback', when the 'receiver' hears and feels criticism. Some individuals can cope with what is clearly criticism and after feeling curious will ask for more detailed or more helpful feedback. Others will respond by either becoming overtly defensive, i.e. giving an aggressive response, or remaining obtusely silent.

Culture, Climate and the Learning Organisation

The emphasis in this chapter so far has been on the help which individuals can consciously provide in helping others to develop. In addition to work at this person to person level, it must be recognized that there are issues and problems which can probably be tackled only on a larger scale, for example, at the organizational level.

One way of tackling the problems has been the creation of management development systems, policies, disciplines and procedures of the kind spelled out in Chapter 9. These are characteristically an attempt to provide a specially organized management development environment in which good development practices are promoted and supported by the organization. If we accept for the moment that many of the policies and disciplines are in fact desirable from the point of view of encouraging development, one of the first issues about what individuals mean by being helped is that they would like to see the theories and policies of an organization put into practice. If the organization proclaims belief in the virtues of at least annual appraisal, they want to be appraised. If the organization believes in an open door policy, they want to be able to walk into that open space to make their contribution. If the organization favours off-the-job training, they want to be sent on courses at appropriate times, they do not want the organization to prevent them from going on the course in the end because of 'pressure of work', and they want to attend the course without a barrage of messages from work requiring their attention to ongoing problems. The first level of help to be provided at the organizational level is that there should be a systematic and disciplined attempt to carry through whatever the organization espouses as its formal management development processes. Efforts to monitor actual performance will indicate some of the defects and gaps in the actual implementation.

We now have as part of our agenda matters above and beyond the management development system. The concept of the organization as a learning system, and moreover a system which encourages learning not just through formal management development processes but by its whole rationale and approach to work, is one which potentially has great power to influence learning. Specifically it has great potential for encouraging managers to act as helpers over a much wider range of processes than simply those of the formal management development system. So the idea of 'The Learning Organization' is one which could increase the totality of effort devoted to the widest range of provision and use of learning opportunities. The evolution of the phrase 'The Learning Organization' has not yet been accompanied by very clear definitions of it, nor by concrete expressions of practices demonstrating what the learning organization is. Except, in the latter case, for those organizations which count their formal management development processes and then believe that they have designed a learning organisation!

If therefore we accept that one of the things which defines what is meant by help is the creation of a Learning Organization, a useful starting point is a definition. Peter Honey and I have produced the definition which is shown in Chart 5.3.

Chart 5.3 Definition of the Learning Organization

'Creating an environment
where the behaviours and practices
involved in continuous development
are actively encouraged.'

Whether or not you choose to adopt this or some other definition, it is what determines whether your organization is actually a Learning Organization or not which is important. Thus our emphasis on the word 'practices'. In our view the Learning Organization is one in which certain methods are encouraged – and where the absence of encouragement reveals that this organization is less than perfect as a learning environment. Again, Honey and I have provided a very detailed questionnaire which enables individuals and organizations to assess this. A less sophisticated but still useful method of checking the extent to which an organization provides encouragement for a learning culture is the checklist which is reproduced with the permission of my fellow author (Chart 5.4).

One More Time – What is Help?

Help is what a learner hears, not what a helper says.

Help is what an individual wants, not necessarily what the individual needs.

Help is delivered by someone believed by the learner to be trying to be helpful rather than damaging.

Help is delivered to and accepted by people whose unique individual characteristics form part of the structure of the help offered.

Help is always defined by what the learner can accept and use, not what the helper can deliver.

Help is facilitated by organizational practices which give support to the best endeavours of well motivated helpers.

EXERCISE 5.4

1. Think of your different roles as boss, mentor, colleague.
2. Think of an individual to whom you have offered help through one of these roles recently.

3. What have been the difficulties in offering accurate, relevant, useful advice?
4. Think of an individual for whom you may have the opportunity of offering advice. What issues will you need to think of?

Chart 5.4   Organizational climate checklist

1. Review each of the following factors for your organization in relation to management development. Mark each factor on a scale of 0=low / 10=high to indicate the extent to which you believe the criterion to be currently met.

My organization encourages learning because:	Score
It encourages managers to identify their own learning needs.	
It provides a regular review of performance and learning for the individual.	
It encourages managers to set challenging learning goals for themselves.	
It provides feedback at the time on both performance and achieved learning.	
It reviews the performance of managers in helping to develop others.	
It assists managers to see learning opportunities on the job.	
It seeks to provide new experiences from which managers can learn.	
It provides or facilitates the use of training off the job.	
It tolerates some mistakes provided managers try to learn from them.	
It encourages managers to review, conclude and plan learning activities.	
It encourages managers to challenge the traditional ways of doing things.	

6

The helping relationship

Different Types of Help

Help starts for most managers with managerial situations and opportunities described in the Introduction and Chapters 2 and 3. The situation creates the opportunity for, and recognition of, the need for help in resolving managerial problems and taking up managerial opportunities. As a link between the last chapter and a review of different kinds of helper, it will be useful to set out the main types of help which may be offered.

Problem Centred

Help derives from and is centred on the opportunities, issues and problems arising in managerial work. The urgency, reality and centrality of managerial performance drive any analysis for discussion. The initial purpose and the continuing prime direction of any discussion is how to define, improve, register and monitor managerial performance. Any help is initially recognized as 'helping to resolve the problem', rather than 'helping you to learn'. The help is accidental, incidental to the managerial process but can have a powerful effect because it centres on issues central to perceptions by managers of what their life is about. 'Jane, let's fix a time to talk through the presentation you made this morning. There are some points about the participants' questions and your answers we need to sort out.'

Awareness of Need

Discussion of managerial opportunities, problems and issues can lead to discussion about managerial styles, behaviour and skills. While such discussions can and often do remain purely centred on the existence or level of required managerial attributes such as skills – or less helpfully personality attributes – the discussion can also begin to move towards a learning and development mode. Thus a failure to understand or to deal with some managerial issue can lead to suggestions about what kind of skill or knowledge an individual needs in order to be able to tackle such issues or problems more successfully.

There is obviously a greater awareness of 'what you need to be able to learn to do'. The identification of such a need and the delivery of statements about it may both be authoritarian rather than participative in tone. Sharp statements can and do sometimes jog people into learning experiences they would not otherwise have. In general, however, explicit statements of 'what you need', rather than discussion about 'what you think has been happening here' will be less helpful. 'What do you think?' creates less defensiveness and encourages thought by the potential learner. 'How well do you think your people get on together?' is more helpful than 'I think you and your people ought to have a Team Development course'.

Awareness of Learning

Least likely to happen for many managers is identification of the explicit learning opportunity contained within managerial activities. The most advanced form of helping is not simply the creation of useful discussions about managerial opportunities and problems, important, realistic and frequent though this is. It is the additional recognition that within these activities learning opportunities exist. Moreover, it is the recognition not of opportunities in general – described earlier as the Big O – but of specific kinds of learning opportunity. In addition, the managerial helpers need to understand for themselves the learning process involved in effective learning, as described in terms of the Learning Cycle (see Chapter 4), and the issue of individual preferences in terms of preferred Learning Styles.

At this stage the importance of this third element should be recognized. Managers, particularly good ones, have presented opportunities for learning in many of the ways given as illustrations in the chapters so far. Good problem centred discussion and creation of awareness of managerial skills has been one of the hallmarks of the ways in which successful managers have helped with the development of others. However, the generally appalling lack of discussion about, and provision of help on, the learning process, means that this has been all too often a well intentioned but small part of the helping relationship. If you do not understand the main features of how managers learn, especially the relationship between how you learn and how others might learn differently, your capacity to help is limited.

Recognition that helping occurs, in different ways, to a varying extent and with different degrees of acceptability is one part of the process of becoming a more effective helper. Of course, one of the intentions of this book is also to encourage a more proactive approach. Not only can we help managers to recognize and make use of the multitude of experiences they have, we can also encourage them to stimulate, and indeed to provide, such experiences. This chapter is concerned particularly with activities driven by, and opportunities that might be recognized by, managers in their normal work situation. In Chapter 9 we look at how these activities can be described and used within the formal development system.

Six Types of Helper

In earlier chapters we have seen four different managerial relationships at work in helping others to learn – boss, mentor, colleagues and subordinates. Two other managerial relationships or roles also help in the development of others:

- **grand boss**, i.e. a manager above the learner's immediate manager;
- **client** or **sponsor**, i.e. a manager for whom a project or task is being undertaken, who is not the boss or grand boss.

Chart 6.1 Six managerial helpers in development

- Grand Boss
- Boss
- Mentor
- Client/Sponsor
- Colleagues
- Subordinates

As we shall in the next chapter, different helpers can have different contributions to make. That chapter extends the range of activities beyond the Problem Centred, Needs and Learning analysis offered above. In this chapter the intention is to establish the broad picture of the six prime roles.

Other Helpers

Although the concentration here is on line relationships within an organization, the range of potential helpers extends beyond this – Figure 6.1 shows this.

Again the emphasis on help in and around the job precludes attention to some of the other people who actually help development. For example:

- domestic partners

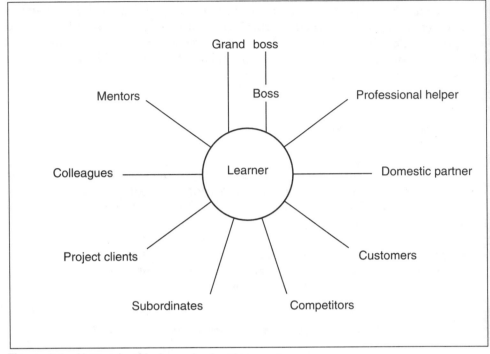

Figure 6.1   Network of helpers in development

- external network
- the people who act as a sounding board or listening ear.

Though each of these may provide valuable help, they do not do so within the managerial relationship which is the subject of this book.

Some people provide unconscious help. Thus clients and customers provide experiences which help learning, not only in the sense of dealing with difficult people or providing opportunities to be successful, but also by providing good models or techniques of managerial behaviour. Competitors can also provide useful opportunities for learning, through observing their successes and failures, their techniques and their relationships with customers.

It may surprise many readers to see the range of people by whom they might be helped. Since management is in most organizations essentially a people centred activity, it ought not to be surprising – it is probably just another of those cases where a manager has not previously been asked to think about the issue, and therefore has not recognized all the contributors on whom it is possible to call.

Before we turn to a more detailed analysis of what each of the managerial helpers provides, readers might like to do an exercise which tests their level of awareness before we make it easier by giving more examples.

EXERCISE 6.1

1. Consider Chart 6.1.
2. Have any of these individuals given you any help on learning from a managerial experience?
3. Has their help been explicitly understood by either of you as being about learning?
4. Or has the help really been 'to understand or do my job better' with a subsequent awareness of what you have learned?
5. Were you aware at the time or very soon afterwards that you had learned something?
6. In what ways has this exercise made you think, perhaps for the first time, about the fact of being helped, what you learned and how you learned it?

Now readers have looked at things from the 'receiving' point of view we turn attention to the 'giving' role.

EXERCISE 6.2

1. Consider Chart 6.1.
2. Have you, operating in one of these roles, recently helped someone else to learn from a managerial experience?
3. Did you set out to help them learn, or did you set out to help improve their managerial effectiveness primarily?
4. How clear was it at the time, do you think, to the person whom you believe you helped?
5. How clear was it at the time to you that you were helping them to learn?
6. Do you think now you could have helped them learn more from the experience if you had understood it more clearly as a learning opportunity?
7. Can you now think of recent cases in which you failed to recognize a learning opportunity, and may have failed to help them to recognize it?

Helpers in Action

In this chapter we are concerned with who the helpers are, and some examples of the help they provide. *How* they provide help is detailed in Chapters 7, 9 and 10. In order to make this chapter self-contained, while avoiding the repetition of the particular examples given in the previous chapter, new examples are given of each of the helpers in action.

Boss

'My boss would take time in joint problem solving to let me reach my own conclusions, letting me go through my own thinking processes. Sometimes this led to outcomes which he probably anticipated. On other occasions an unexpected solution emerged and he would say "That's interesting" and be prepared to develop it. He worked hard at problem solving, able to think laterally and find answers to questions which seemed sometimes impossible to me to solve. I learned a lot from working with him, and from his explanations of the techniques he favoured in this area.'

Grand Boss

James E. Burke of the massively successful American company, Johnson and Johnson, quotes an experience in a book by Thomas Horton. He was congratulated by General Johnson on a failed project that cost nearly $1 million (at a time when that figure was worth a great deal more than now). General Johnson told him 'Don't make the same mistake again, but you cannot make decisions without making mistakes'.

There are three issues worth mentioning here since we have not talked about the grand boss before. The first is that long before present understandings of 'The Learning Organization', General Johnson was providing an environment in which people were not frightened to learn. The second was that James Burke learned from the mistake. The third point is that he learned from the way in which General Johnson handled the mistake and his own involvement with it.

Mentor

'A lot of my development is due to a man I never actually worked for. He was actually twenty years older than me and worked in a different function in the organization. We originally met quite accidentally playing tennis. He was such an open, friendly guy that I asked him a few questions about something that was going on in our organization that I found worrying. After that, we developed a habit of talking to each other from time to time. I discussed possible assignments and even job moves with him and I know in at least one case he contributed to the decision that I should arrange to work on a particular project. But the most helpful thing really was that he would give me half an hour to discuss some of the new things I was involved with.'

Colleagues

'My current management team is the best I have ever worked in. We have different backgrounds and experiences which is tremendously productive when it comes to both creating ideas and then deciding what to do. For example, I was recently being considered for a job in another country. One of my colleagues went over his experience of working there for another organization. It was like having a tutorial about the realities of managing abroad.'

Subordinate

'One of my subordinates came up with a quite different approach to the big decisions that we have to make from time to time. Not the smaller things where experience and a feel for the business really means that you don't have to do a tremendous analytical job. But on some of the really crucial things he suggested a way of going about the decision process that was really an eye-opener to me. He had picked it up from a course he had been on, used it himself before he came to work for me, so I felt fairly confident that it was a valid process – and it turned out to work very well.'

Project Client or Sponsor

'I was asked to work on a project which looked at the Purchasing arrangements in our company. I was not a purchasing specialist – I worked in the department that mainly used the results. We had some pretty strong views about what we thought were the inefficiencies of their arrangement, the cost and the time it sometimes took so that we were held up. Perhaps I had talked about too much in too many places and that was why I was given the project. The client was a director who had responsibility for a number of different functions including purchasing. I am sure he actually stopped me doing what might have been a bad job. He went to a lot of trouble to establish with me what the objectives of the project were, what the boundaries were and how I might cross them, who I would have to see and how I might handle them. Then towards the end of the project he gave me a real jolt by asking me what the criteria for success were in relation to the report I was going to submit. What I learned from carrying out that project for him has made me insistent ever since on the need to set objectives and standards for performance. It is easy to spend your time being busy as a manager; you have to think hard if you want to be effectively busy.'

A Word on Definitions

With the exception of grand boss – my own invention – the titles in my chart are familiar and well understood. There is a problem with one of them, mentor. Both management vocabulary and management development literature have allowed a confusing integration of two roles which are in fact quite different. Much of the American literature on mentors in fact describes work carried out by and help given by bosses in relation to their subordinates.

What a boss provides, how it is provided, for what purpose and with what level of responsibility is quite different from what a mentor does. Even when the mentor is formally appointed as part of a management development process, the relationship of mentor to the learning manager does not contain the crucial elements of accountability and the involvement of the boss in the results of whether the subordinate has learned effectively or not. It is, for example, much easier for a mentor to discuss a problem involving a failure of performance in judicious, balanced and objective terms than it is for a boss whose own career may be affected by the failure of a subordinate.

This book therefore applies the term 'mentor' to someone who has no direct management responsibility for the manager who is learning.

EXERCISE 6.3

Now you can go back to the first two exercises in this chapter and reconsider them in the light of these additional examples. You may also wish to return to pages 83–5 to consider the examples given there which may similarly help you see situations in which you have been involved.

Can you now add to the answers you gave to Exercises 6.1 and 6.2?

A Continuum of Helping Relationships

In this chapter so far we have been centred entirely on situations in which help has been given through job-centred activities. Of course, all the roles spelled out in this chapter can also form part of a structured formal management development process. How this can be encouraged, created and directed through a management development policy and its associated activities is discussed in Chapters 9 and 10. Here we continue with an explanation of the different kind of relationship which exists between each of the 'Six Helpers' and the 'Learning Manager', described in terms of their direct managerial relationship as distinct from their management development relationship.

The nature of that managerial relationship can be seen on a continuum related to the strength of the managerial authority involved. The closest relationship clearly is that between the managerial learner and boss or grand boss. The paradox here is that the very closeness of the managerial relationship can on the one hand help with clear identification of learning opportunities and achieved learning, but can also hinder because of a relatively narrow focus on 'let's get the job done'.

Next on the continuum is the client for a project or task force. Rather similar considerations apply here in the sense of a shared prime concern for achievement of the task or project. However, a slightly less intense and continuous managerial relationship may mean that there is more space for discussion of issues, problems and therefore learning.

Chart 6.2   A continuum related to managerial authority

High managerial authority over learner	Informal authority	No managerial authority over learner
Boss Grand boss Client	Mentor	Colleagues Subordinates

The mentor, since he or she is in my definition removed from a direct line relationship, potentially has a particularly productive helping relationship. No longer so personally concerned with managerial achievement, in the sense of potentially being blamed for any failure of the junior manager, the mentor can and does focus more on facilitating learning opportunities and discussing learning achievement. There is no *managerial* authority in the organizational sense – there is usually a *feeling* of authority due to status, experience and wisdom.

Colleagues clearly have a different relationship because of the kind of help they may offer. Indeed, of course, some colleagues offer the reverse of help both managerially and in learning! If, however, we take the positive situations, colleagues can provide, at their best, opportunities for discussion and feedback which, again at its best, can be direct, immediate, job centred but not determinative in career terms. Of course like all the others they can provide feedback which is not helpful and Chapter 7 discusses the skills, behaviours and attitudes necessary for any of these to provide effective help.

Finally, subordinates can be helpers. In managerial authority, this is in effect a reverse of the first three helpers above – since they do not have authority over the person being helped. It is precisely this factor which, of course, makes the helping relationship between a boss and subordinate potentially and actually rather fraught. While objectively and rationally it is possible to recognize what an intelligent subordinate might provide, protection of one's managerial ego and authority often means that the kind of listening exchange which would actually help the more senior manager is peculiarly difficult to achieve. Chart 6.2 sets out the continuum.

EXERCISE 6.4   AUTHORITY AND A HELPING RELATIONSHIP

1. Consider the 'Six Helpers'.
2. Think of a recent occasion on which you have been involved in a managerial activity with at least one of them.
3. Has your capacity to work with them, and to understand fully the issues involved, been affected by the nature of the authority relationship?
4. Has your capacity to learn from the activity been affected by the relationship?
5. Now that you have undertaken this analysis, can you think of ways in

which you could, on some occasions, put aside the authority issue, and learn more effectively from the activity?

Managerial Style and the Helping Relationship

The way a manager, especially a boss, behaves in the normal managerial situations profoundly affects the kind of help she or he can give, and the receptivity of the learner. The 'normal situation' managerial behaviours most likely to encourage a managerial learner are set out in Chart 6.3.

Chart 6.3   Managerial behaviours facilitating learning

- a democratic/participative decision making style
- the ability to listen
- the ability to plan ahead
- the ability to give explicit direct feedback
- the skill of providing feedback at a time when it is not only appropriate but capable of being used
- the ability to engage in processes of questioning, reflecting and planning what to do next
- the ability to listen and reflect, rather than give direct statements such as 'what you should have learned from that is'
- the ability to be a good role model – to show how to learn by personal demonstration, rather than just by excitation about how someone else should learn
- the capacity to share understanding of the total learning process
- the ability to recognize learning opportunities within the prime managerial activity

These managerial behaviours are, with the exception of the last two, valuable managerial skills, recognizably drawn from the familiar managerial world. Of course, there is a more specific list of skills manager helpers need to be able to deploy in the developmental role. They are described in the next chapter. The intention here is to emphasize the extent to which managers can be helpful in the way in which they manage without putting on a special developmental style.

EXERCISE 6.5   WHAT ARE MY CHARACTERISTICS AS A HELPER?

1. Review the list of characteristics given in Chart 6.3 above.
2. Give yourself a score on a scale 0 = I am not good at this, 10 = I am very good at this, for each characteristic.
3. Consider someone with whom you have a managerial relationship, and whose learning you might be currently helping.
4. How helpful you do think you have actually been in relation to some recent managerial activity?
5. Consider your score in general, and your response to the previous question.

6. Do you think the individual or individuals involved would give you a better, or a worse, score?
7. Do you think you might need to improve in your ability to perform on some of these characteristics?
8. If so, make some notes on one or two areas in which you might improve in preparation for reading the next chapter.

The kind of learning achieved by one person from another may not be secured by the kind of positive relationship suggested by the desirable list of characteristics. In practice, managers often mention points they have learned from and with other people which are not initially obvious as being helpful learning experiences. You can, for example, have as a boss someone who is a negative role model, who shows you exactly how things should not be done. Since this book is about positive aspects of the helping relationship, designed for people who would actually want to improve their ability to help, this point is not pursued here.

A Special Word on Colleagues

It is important to emphasize the potential contribution of colleagues since they are not covered in later chapters. This relationship has many similarities to that of the mentor in the psychological issues involved. As with the mentor there is a non-authority basis, which removes some potential problems. Emphasis can now be given to a relatively relaxed relationship, based around mutual help rather than performance requirement dictated by authority relationships.

Colleagues can provide emotional support, personal feedback, friendship – a relationship which is driven more by personal feelings than by managerial requirements. However, as the cases involving colleagues quoted so far in this book indicate, there are situations in which the helping relationship is centred more on particular managerial problems and issues. The colleague may provide help in learning about leadership style, how they affect other people, how others are performing and particularly how a mutual boss is acting.

In my experience colleagues give and receive much more help than the managerial literature has recognized. Indeed, giving and receiving is, of course, the special feature of the relationship. Whereas, as we indicated with the 'hotel case' (Chapter 3), a manager can learn, although rather differently, from the same situation in which he is helping someone else to learn, the nature of the exchange is predominantly not one of mutuality. With colleagues, however, there is likely to be more equal exchange. One colleague may be better than you at one kind of work or be seized with a different level of skill, or have a different mental or psychological approach. You, in turn, may have equivalent but different things to offer. While overall, therefore, the

Principle of Reciprocity operates to a greater degree in all helping relationships than we have often recognized, colleagues provide the clearest case of reciprocal benefits.

The relationship between colleagues depends on what each can offer and what each wants. A broad categorization is as follows.

Sharing Information

Managers learn by acquiring information from other people - hence the general power of the managerial network. From colleagues they acquire information about issues, problems, forecasts about organizational changes and statements about difficulties arising. Some colleagues are particularly good at, and indeed seem to be dedicated towards, providing information to their colleagues. I had a colleague in one organization who was said to know more about a greater range of things going on in the organization than any other collection of four people put together. He was an important person to know, and an important person to use. There was a down side to any relationship with him – he knew so much because he was dedicated to acquiring the knowledge. It was difficult to have a discussion with him on some things unless you actually wanted that information to be shared with a wider group!

Problem Discussing Colleagues

My research and experience shows that there are colleagues whom we deliberately seek out to discuss particular problems. This may be because of their knowledge or their skill or because the particular situation demands it, or because we just think it is a good way of influencing others towards our point of view. We learn from them because they have experience, knowledge or skills we do not possess to the same degree. We learn from them because they have a different perspective. We learn from them because they tell us things either from direct observation about our own performance, or they tell us what they have heard from others about our performance.

Emotionally Supportive Colleagues

We go to other colleagues not so much for information, not so much for performance related discussion, but because they provide warmth and emotional support – in other words friendship. These are the most intimate colleagues with whom we discuss our dilemmas, difficulties and often our deepest feelings. With them we finally reach the most difficult area for most managers – confession, discussion and receiving absolution for our internal vulnerabilities. With them we share our disasters and failures in colourful, explicit and cathartic detail. Such relationships take time to develop, are usually approached with delicacy through one kind of sharing to see whether your colleague can offer you something and also, of course, to see whether you can trust that this sharing between the two of you will not become sharing with a wider range of people (note the difference from the information sharing colleagues mentioned first above).

Colleagues can create a conscious learning partnership by the open exchange of experiences with the explicit intention of learning.

EXERCISE 6.6   COLLEAGUES AS HELPERS

1. Do you recognize a relationship with any of your colleagues of any of the types mentioned above?
2. With which colleagues do you have what kind of relationship?
3. With which of them do you think you are primarily helping them?
4. With which of them do you think they are primarily helping you?
5. Do you now recognize possibilities for helping or being helped, not currently being used?
6. Can you select now someone to whom you might offer more help, or from whom you might receive it?

Back to the Boss

The final word on the manager as developer of others must go to the person in the most influential role, for most learners – the boss. The boss is involved in the most significant managerial situations, and has the authority not only to initiate but to influence discussion on development opportunities and solutions. Further discussion of ways in which bosses can use these opportunities will be found in Chapters 7–10.

7
Helping individuals to learn

So far, we have looked at:

When – the situations in which help can be provided (see Chapters 1–3)
Why – the processes by which needs for help can be identified (see Chapters 1–3. Also see Chapters 9–10 on more formal processes)
Who – the people who may provide help (see Chapter 4).

Now we turn to:

How – help can be provided by line managers (suggestions for the kind of help which might be provided by professional advisers on development are given in the Appendix).

There are two issues which need to be recognized before considering the detail of how help is to be provided. These are the centrality of the person to be helped, and the perceptions by managers of their existing behaviour.

The first consideration has already been given on pages 67–8:

Help is defined by the learner not by the helper.

The second consideration, the perception by managers of their own managerial behaviour, attaches slightly different words to the song frequently sung already in this book. Much effective development emerges from what managers do in and around their jobs. When we look at the themes, or, to continue the musical analogy, the lyrics of this chapter, we see that again managers are already engaged in the developmental process built around the job. They help people to learn by 'talking through the problem with them', 'discussing over a drink how their future career might develop', 'going over a presentation with her the day before she was due to make it'. Managers who have a deserved reputation for developing the people around them carry out more of these activities obviously than managers who, equally deservedly, are known to be poor at helping other people to develop. In an attempt to improve the practices of even the better developmental managers, and to start other managers in the use of more effective helping processes, formal management development systems have appropriated terms which originate outside management, and are rarely used by managers themselves. Formal management development activity in terms of the personal help given by one manager to another is often described as 'coaching' and 'mentoring'. Instead of leaping into the use of these terms it is more sensible to start from where managers are, to look at the ways in which they are experienced in helping others, and only then to look at whether words and processes such as coaching or mentoring are useful.

In my research on management development I have found that in the UK managers relatively rarely talk about being coached or mentored. If they do it is usually a reference back to an early experience in management. (Research in the USA suggests a rather different picture, but this is because the term 'mentor' there includes the role of the boss which, as I argued in Chapter 6, confuses two different roles.) Managers do not characteristically see themselves as having operated as coaches or mentors, nor do they see themselves as having been helped by coaches and mentors. When they describe themselves as having been helped by other people they do not generally attach a role to the statement, but describe a process. What they describe is what I call 'mutual problem solving'. They will talk about an individual, or a group of individuals, who offered assistance on a particular problem, opportunity, situation or task (see Chapters 2 and 3). One example may remind readers of the many illustrations given earlier:

> 'We had a difficult problem to negotiate with another division in the company. I had been working on this with some colleagues, and we went into my boss with our proposed answer. I was a few sentences into my explanation of our proposal when he told me he had read the paper from which I was speaking. "You don't need to convince me; we have to convince him. I'll be Jack Green, now you set about convincing me". So I was into a role play.'

In describing this event to me, the individual concerned, in response to an earlier question in the interview, had said that he could never remember having been coached in his managerial work. Yet when asked to describe some of the events through which he had learned he came up with the example given above. Like the Frenchman introduced for the first time to the difference between poetry and prose, who commented that he had not realized that he had been speaking prose all his life, most managers would not recognize that they had coached or been coached. They are aware of their constant involvement in tackling their managerial responsibilities, in the course of which they offer help and are given help.

Here is an example of a different kind of involvement:

'When I was first appointed as a manager, X was my boss's boss. After I had worked under him for a year, he moved onto other things. But we encountered each other from time to time even though we worked in different areas of the organization. He always wanted to know what I was doing, what the interesting issues and problems were. We would have dinner together sometimes. I would phone him up and ask for his advice on some issues. He was particularly helpful in my earlier days about politics – how to go about influencing important people.'

In this case the manager concerned was uncomfortable when I suggested that X had been his mentor. 'He was just a nice guy, more experienced than I was, who took an interest in me. Mentor makes it sound more formal than I am sure either of us thought it was. No-one asked him to take up this relationship with me as far as I know – and certainly no-one suggested to me that he should be my mentor.'

Discussions with managers often produce reactions such as 'I do it anyway – why do you need to give me different words for it?'; 'You are adding another of those fancy management development techniques to my work – I don't have enough time to do my job as it is'. So one possibility would simply be to remind managers that in the course of their normal work they will have opportunities to help other people perform their tasks more effectively, through mutual problem solving and the associated communication, questioning, advising and knowledge giving likely to be involved in the process. Indeed that is the best place to start – which is why this chapter looks first at what managers already do. However, as in other areas of development, what managers already do is often insufficient, inefficient and ineffective if left in its purely natural state. The case for identifying what is involved in helping others more clearly, and for applying specific words to those activities, is that this:

- sharpens awareness
- clarifies the requirements
- leads to the identification and improvement of the skills required.

Starting from Where You Are

A number of organizations have set up formal programmes encouraging managers to act as coach or mentor, and providing guidance for them on how to carry out these roles. The justification for this has just been mentioned – clarifying roles, setting organizational expectations, and providing skills, training and the exercise of the role leads to improved performance. However soundly based such programmes are in organizational requirements, and especially in the elements of formal management development, the starting point for managers should be their experience of carrying out these activities in terms that they understand. A manager who wants to help others to learn should not be asked to think first of coaching or mentoring, but rather to think about situations in which help might be offered, and about needs that might be met. This is to start from where the manager is – the strongly felt imperative to improve individual or group performance. If the concepts of coaching and mentoring are introduced too soon to the manager, without attempting to construct them on the basis of existing recognized experience, the danger is that immediately they are seen as management development practices rather than managerial practices. However, once that ground rock of experience has been recognized and used, the concepts and techniques involved in giving effective help to individuals can be presented, discussed and implemented. The formal identification of helping activities adds to the range of what is being offered. This is illustrated in Chart 7.1.

Chart 7.1 illustrates two points. First, managers tend to express the help they are offering in a colloquial form. Second, the formal helping processes identify more clearly a greater number of helping activities.

Chart 7.1　Managers help individuals

Informally Through
Problem solving
Here is how to . . .
What do you think about . . .?
Let's talk about your job
Delegating effectively
Here is a chance for you to learn something
What do you reckon is the way you learn best?
Would you like some feedback on that?
Let's get together and you tell me what you really think
What do you think you might learn on project/new job?
What did you pick up through that experience?

Formally Through
Coaching
Mentoring
Counselling
Defining the job
Setting task objectives and priorities
Reviewing performance
Identifying learning opportunities
Describing the Learning and Cycle Styles
Selecting the right method for learning
Creating a Personal Development Plan/Learning Contract
Undertaking a learning review

Who Provides What Help?

The list of direct helpers offered in Chapter 6 was:

Grand Boss
Boss
Mentor
Client/Sponsor
Colleagues
Subordinates

The central feature of the process is the individual learner. In saying that the definition of help is provided by the learner and not by the helper, we also need to add that the contribution of self is fundamental to the exercise in a practical and not merely a psychological sense. Effective help must be based on a learner's self-assessment, not just the helper's analysis. Then together helper and learner generate joint commitment to working to a jointly agreed plan, which, like any management plan, must then be reviewed in assessing progress.

The list of activities in Chart 7.1 is too extensive to set about listing the contributions by particular helpers in a way which is usable by managers. In summarized form, some of the activities carried out or not carried out by individual helpers are shown in Chart 7.2.

Chart 7.2   Helpers and their roles

	Problem solving	Coaching	Mentoring	Counselling	Performance review and needs	Manager in dev. system	Learning to learn
Grand boss	X	X	–	X	X	X	X
Boss	X	X	–	X	X	X	X
Mentor	X	X	X	X	–	½	X
Colleague	X	½	X	X	?	–	?
Subordinate	X	–	–	–	–	–	?
Project client	½	–	–	–	X	–	–
Self	X	?	?	?	X	X	X

Why Do I Give Help?

It was suggested earlier that the normal situation in which managers offer or receive help derives from the managerial imperative of getting work done effectively. In some organizations, in addition, it was suggested the formal management development process invites or instructs individuals to provide help. At the most general level the reasons why one individual manager offers help to another are:

1. If I help her to do her job more effectively, it reduces the problems coming across my desk.
2. The management development system tells me that I should find opportunities to help my people by personal action.

A third stimulus also operates. Most managers actually enjoy working with other people and gain satisfaction from relationships. (Of course, many of them could find more satisfaction in a greater level of achievement – one of the purposes of development!) For at least some managers some of the time the stimulus for offering help is the feeling of personal satisfaction involved in the development of other individuals. In addition to the stimulus provided by performance improvement for the boss's own reasons, or actions undertaken to satisfy the requirements of a management development scheme, some managers engage in helping others simply because they derive satisfaction from doing so – the rewards are intrinsic to themselves rather than extrinsic (created by the situational system). This is another manifestation of the Principle of Reciprocity at work – a return to the helper from the experience of helping.

EXERCISE 7.1   WHY MIGHT I WANT TO HELP?

Think of some big situations, or smaller activities, in which someone you know at work is involved, and on which you might be able to help them.

1. Why might you want to help them? (Consider the points made earlier in this chapter.)
2. What do you think the balance of benefit will be to you, to the learner, or to the organization generally?
3. What aspects of the working environment might encourage you to give help, and what aspects might constrain you?
4. Are you most likely to offer help in an informal situation, i.e. entirely between you and individual?
5. Are there circumstances in which you might be undertaking this within your organization's formal management development system?
6. What experience do you have in offering the kind of help you envisage?
7. Have you received formal training in acting as a mentor or coach?

EXERCISE 7.2   SELECTING AN INDIVIDUAL FOR HELP

1. Think of an individual to whom you might offer help.
2. What are your reasons for choosing that person?
3. What situations/activities/tasks indicate that the individual might respond to help?
4. What specific learning opportunities do you think might arise within those situations/activities/tasks?
5. What process might you use to discuss what you will attempt?
6. What criteria for success might you be able to suggest?
7. What kind of review process could you set up?
8. How does your proposal fit into the rest of the formal management development system?

EXERCISE 7.3   MY EXPERIENCE AS A HELPER

Consider the range of possibilities shown in Chart 7.2 on page 97.

1. In which of these categories have you had experience as a helper?

2. In which category do you think your help has been most effective?
3. In which category are you proposing to operate (see your answers to Exercise 7.2 above)?
4. Consider your personal style, skill and characteristics as a helper. Which things have contributed to your success as a helper?
5. Consider your personal style, skill and characteristics as a helper. Are there any characteristics which may have hindered your capacity to help someone else?

Different Styles of Help

Much of the existing literature on this subject, especially when discussing the formal mentoring and coaching roles, emphasizes a non-directive, reflective style orientated to a listening manager as a helper. There are two problems with this. The first is that this suggests a style of behaviour which is quite foreign to a lot of managers. Secondly, it tends to suggest as a basic style something which is appropriate to some circumstances but not to others. The reason for a manager being in the position to offer help to someone else is the possession of greater knowledge, skill, experience or insight. Although in the list of skills given below reflective and listening skills therefore form a part, it is essential to recognize that there are circumstances in which the helping manager actually tells someone else what to do and how to do it. One of the skills of the coach or mentor, or of the problem solving helper, lies precisely in identifying those occasions when it is appropriate to lay things out for an individual, as compared with those where, with more effort and a little more time, greater understanding can be secured through drawing things out.

Some Characteristics of an Effective Helping Relationship

Once the prospective helper has established that help is defined by the learner rather than by the helper, an implicit definition of the kind of relationship which should exist can be developed. Indeed, of course, it can be explicitly agreed between the helper and the learner. The characteristics set out in Chart 7.3 apply to all the situations discussed in this chapter.

Point 7 can be expanded. Managers will quite frequently claim to have learned something even from bad bosses. Basically, of course, they learn how not to do things. Sometimes they learn from an experience, some demonstration of skill where a boss has a competence which may stand out, like a good deed in a naughty world. While it is possible to learn from observing how an otherwise bad boss behaves, that capacity to learn is not necessarily inhibited by other aspects of how that particular manager performs. It may be inhibited, but for some individuals clearly is not. When we look at the helping relationship, it is improbable that, in the kind of sensitive relationship which needs to exist, a learner will accept help from someone whose management style and attitude contradicts the style, form and content of the help being offered.

Chart 7.3   Characteristics of an effective helping relationship

1. The learner defines what is effective help.
2. The learner may ask for help or the helper may offer it.
3. Informal help revolving around problem solving may not be explicit to start with, but may nonetheless be reviewed after the helping event.
4. Within formal coaching and mentoring situations, a learning contract or agreement needs to be mutually established.
5. Compatibility of sex, age and racial origin are most likely to produce the most effective helper/learner relationship.
6. Mutual understanding of the Task Cycle, Learning Cycle and preferred Learning Styles contributes to an effective learning relationship.
7. Generally a helper/learner relationship can only exist within a broader relationship of credibility, respect and mutual understanding. The attempt to create a learning relationship where the normal managerial relationship is unsatisfactory is for most purposes largely a waste of time.

What is a Coach?

When operating as a coach, a manager consciously guides someone else towards more effective performance through a planned learning process.

As already suggested, the way in which the manager provides guidance can range from a substantially reflective listening mode to a more direct instructional mode. The coaching may be directed at:

- helping someone else solve a problem
- improving a behaviour
- adding to knowledge or insight.

As we shall see immediately below, coaching, by contrast to mentoring, is:

- more likely to be short term than long term in focus
- more likely to be specific rather than general
- more likely to be orientated to performance requirements
- more likely to take place within the organization
- more likely to be delivered by a manager's manager, rather than a colleague or mentor
- more likely to be centred on a specific skill or competence
- most likely to be driven by a combination of needs understood by the individual, the coach and the organization to meet performance requirements.

Skills of the Coach and Problem Solving Helper

Compared with a mentor, a coach or problem solving helper concentrates on a more restricted, though very important, range of issues, and the skills are therefore rather more specific. One reaction to any list of coaching skills is that it is 'just what you would expect any good manager to have'. The point of identifying them, of course, is that while all good managers ought to have all the necessary skills, a number of good managers are not possessed of all the skills at the right level and right quality – and coaching is one example of this. There is widespread agreement on the kind of skills involved. BP Chemicals have a list, reproduced with their permission in Chart 7.4, to which I have added the last two skills.

Chart 7.4   Skills in effective coaching

Active listening	paying full attention, banishing any distractions
Reflective listening	reflecting back to the speaker what you have heard but in your own words to clear up misunderstandings immediately, force them to analyse his or her own ideas, and show that you are listening actively
Open listening	listening with an open mind suspending your judgement to let the individual work an idea through
Drawing out	encouraging the individual to talk about their ideas, feelings and aspirations, helping by asking open questions
Recognizing and revealing feelings	identifying the feelings of others and yourself and being able to talk about them
Giving feedback	giving clear reaction to specific behaviour with sensitivity, in a constructive way and being non-defensive when receiving feedback about your role as coach
Agreeing goals	making sure that each side of the partnership understands what they have to do
Deciding which Coaching Style to use	● a questioning leading to reflection approach ● a questioning leading to challenge approach ● an instructional approach.
Adapting to preferred Learning Styles	

As suggested earlier, the list in Chart 7.4 emphasizes the non-directive, reflective and listening aspects of effective coaching. In many organizations it is probably right to encourage managers to use the reflective approach more often, rather than to allow them to continue to adopt a coaching style which is essentially 'I tell, you follow'. This is one of the areas in which formal management development processes have veered away from some of the realities of management where 'I tell' may be appropriate.

Having made this point in order better to illustrate reality, and to balance the attention paid to non-directive coaching, there is a question which will assist the prospective helper to decide what mode to adopt: 'Will the person learn more if I use a "tell" style, or if I use a "drawing out" style?'

It will be evident that because coaching is essentially concerned with improving performance, and because the problem solving helper is concerned informally to develop performance, the skills necessary for carrying out the helping role under either label are the same. What may be different are the contexts, the motivations of both parties and the feelings of reality or unreality involved. The value, for the problem solving helper, of the coaching list is that it provides a sensible and convenient check on whether, in helping an individual to resolve a problem, help has been offered in a style which both produces a resolution of the problem and also development of the individual.

EXERCISE 7.4   MY SKILLS AS A COACH/PROBLEM SOLVING HELPER

1.   Review the list of skills given in Chart 7.4.
2.   Select a situation in much you believe you have helped someone learn.
3.   Do you perceive yourself as having acted in a problem solving mode (improving performance) or a coaching mode (improving performance through explicit learning)?
4.   On a scale 0 = low on this skill, 10 = high on this skill, how would you assess your own performance?
5.   Do you feel your skills were appropriate to the situation?
6.   If you are not satisfied with your assessment of the skills required in this situation, what actions could you take now?

Case Study 1

A manager has working for him a specialist in business and strategic planning. The specialist has a degree in economics, and achievements recognized in the current organization and in two previous jobs held. The perception of the stategist within the team is that he is an arrogant person never interested in the ongoing problems of the team and the organization, only concerned to relate everything to whether the strategy chosen last year was right. His interventions in meetings, the memos he writes and his direct conversations with individuals are all characterized by the recipients as being 'he thinks he is the only one who understands the business'. The strategist is less arrogant in dealing with his manager, whom he apparently recognizes as his intellectual equal. The manager describes the strategist as being an excellent worker, very productive, and intellectually a good balance with the rest of the team who tend to concentrate on day-to-day issues. However, he does wish that the strategist's relationship with others was better, and believes this might be achieved if he were more prepared to look at things from the point of view of other people rather than just himself.

The manager decides that this is a problem to which he will now give some attention. He proposes to sit down with the strategist to review the problem and work out, if he can, some agreed answers. He has discussed the issue with a Personnel colleague and finds, slightly to his surprise, that what he is proposing to do is coaching. What issues are present here? What skills of coaching are likely to be particularly required?

What is a Mentor?

Since, as we see below, there are a variety of purposes in mentoring, there are also a variety of definitions. Some alternatives are:

- 'Influential people who significantly help you reach your major life goals.'
- Mentoring is 'a process in which one person (mentor) is responsible for overseeing the career and development of another person (protégé) outside the normal manager/subordinate relationship'.

My own definition is:

- A protected relationship in which experimentation, exchange and learning can occur, and skills, knowledge and insight can be developed.

As compared with the coaching role, mentors:

- are often, though not always, concerned with the longer term
- are more likely to be concerned with general issues of jobs, careers and personal growth
- are more interested in general aspects of performance on a broad front, or a few selected items of major significance, rather than the wide range of more detailed performance issues potentially addressed by a coach
- can be within the organization, or outside it
- are more interested in issues of general direction rather than solving immediate problems.

The potential objectives for mentoring include:

- performance
- personal growth
- career development.

These objectives are indicated by the wide range of roles possible under the umbrella-title of mentor (see Chart 7.5).

While any of the roles in Chart 7.5 could be deployed by a mentor, it is

Chart 7.5   Roles of mentors

- Door opener/broker/advocate
- Coach
- Counsellor
- Adviser
- Sounding board/listening post
- Guide
- Role model
- Tutor
- Provider of information/knowledge/wisdom
- Provider of managerial and/or emotional support
- Confronter of problems, behaviours and relationships.

important to establish for any specific helping relationship which of these, or which combination of them, it is hoped to apply with a learner.

Finally, there is the question of whether any manager at any age or level of seniority might be responsive to a mentor as helper. Most of the literature is directed at newcomers to a profession, to management or to high-fliers, for example, people on an MBA programme. My own research with directors, however, showed that a few of them did have a mentor, but always outside their existing organization. Examples of use with young professionals can be found in the now well established requirement within the Institution of Mechanical Engineers that each new young professional in order to complete his or her qualification has to have a mentor, and that mentor must provide an assessment. The Institute of Personnel Management is currently piloting a mentor scheme on a significantly different basis, since it is not required to complete the qualification, nor does it include an assessment. The pilot scheme involves mentor and learner agreeing to meet for 1½ hours a month over a two-year period with a Learning Contract. Further reference to the issue of assessment in relation to coaching and mentoring is given at the end of the chapter.

Case Study 2

Jane is the first woman to have reached her current managerial level in her organization. She is, in addition, the first woman her boss has ever had working for him. He is extremely dominant and tries to conceal chauvinist attitudes under a veneer of public school charm. Jane feels this is not a problem she, as a very new manager, is able to tackle her boss directly on. She knows from other conversations that her 'grand boss' would expect her to resolve her own problems. She knows that other women in the organization are also looking to see how she will handle the issue.

Another manager, senior to herself, but equivalent in status to her boss, has been present at a number of meetings with them. After a meeting he expresses sympathy to Jane and says: 'If I could be helpful in talking over some of the problems with you, I would be glad to try and help. My daughter went through some of the same problems you are experiencing in another organisation.' Jane is being offered help by someone who could be a mentor. What issues are involved here? Are there special factors involved where a potential mentor is of a different sex from the potential learner?

Characteristics of Effective Mentors

David Clutterbuck, who has led the field in the UK on this subject, has developed an excellent list. I have added the last three characteristics to his original characteristics (Chart 7.6).

Chart 7.6 Characteristics of effective mentors

- Already has a good record for developing other people
- Has a genuine interest in seeing younger people advance and can relate to their problems
- Has a wide range of current skills to pass on
- Has a good understanding of the organization, how it works and where it is going
- Combines patience with good interpersonal skills and an ability to work in an unstructured programme
- Has sufficient time to devote to the relationship
- Can command a protégé's respect
- Has his own network of contacts and influence
- Has credibility as a manager
- Has an understanding of the different learning processes available and the different learning preferences of individuals
- Is capable of managing his or her own learning style preferences to provide a successful learning relationship with a protégé.

EXERCISE 7.5 MY CHARACTERISTICS AS A MENTOR

If you currently act as a mentor, either formally or informally, or plan to do so, review the list given above.

1. On a scale 0–10 assess your own score on each of the characteristics.
2. Review a past experience of mentoring, either formally or informally, your beliefs about its effectiveness, and the scores you have given yourself.
3. What conclusions do you draw from this analysis?
4. Think ahead to a prospective mentoring relationship, with a particular individual.

5. Which of your strongest characteristics are likely to be most helpful in the relationship, and which of your weaker characteristics might inhibit it?
6. What if anything can you do to make best use of your strengths and reduce the impact of your weaknesses?

Because of the range of possible roles and objectives contained within the word 'mentor', this list of characteristics can be useful in helping an individual to decide whether to offer help as a mentor – and of course it can suggest to organizations whom they should choose to be mentors within the formal system.

Claire Breeze of the Centre for Action Learning has worked with the Scottish Prison Service to produce some excellent material on mentoring. Some of this is reproduced with her permission as Charts 7.7 and 7.8.

Chart 7.7 Mentors – Creating a learning climate for the learner

Promoting Learning:

- Encouraging Learners to plan opportunities from which to learn.
- Support Learners in risk-taking activities where a benefit to their learning is clear and the organization will not be harmed.
- Deal with Learners' mistakes in a way that is helpful to their understanding rather than punitive.
- Seek opportunities that the Learner may be unaware of to develop their learning capability.
- Encourage Learners to reflect on their experiences and draw conclusions from them.

What is Problem Solving Help?

The argument in this chapter has been that the formal roles, particularly attached to the words 'mentor' and 'coach', originate from a variety of informal activities in which one manager helps another in resolving problems. It was suggested earlier that one of the differences is that the manager helping through problem solving probably has not negotiated a learning contract with the learner – almost certainly they will not use the words 'helper' and 'learner'. The problem solving helper in fact may carry out any of the roles of coach or mentor, in relation to any of the objectives mentioned above. There is no separate and discrete list appropriate only to the problem solver. What the problem solver needs is recognition that, when carrying out any of those roles with any of those objectives, a movement is occurring from a substantially task centred approach to the fellow manager. The role shifts first to one which is, at least partially, centred on learning and development, through to one where the relationship is primarily one of learning and development, to which the terms 'mentor' and 'coach' can then properly be applied.

Chart 7.8 Mentors' behaviours, measures and standards

At mentor meeting, ask learner to articulate possible learning opportunities on the job as he/she sees them.

Share in and support the creation of learning plans with the learner.

Each mentor meeting should raise at least one new learning opportunity to explore.

Identify explicitly with the learner what possible risks are involved in a potential learning route, e.g. fear of failure, risk to safety.

Be explicit in your support once you have both satisfied the ratio of benefits to risk.

Explore the mistakes made in a way that encourages learning by listening, praising positive elements where possible and posing questions like 'What have you learned?' 'What would you do differently next time?'

Be willing to admit to your own mistakes in this relationship and share what you have learned with your learner at regular intervals or when asked.

Offer other routes of learning that the learner seems to neglect, avoid and be unaware of, e.g. looking out for good examples of good practice within the organization.

Keep an informal record of the *ways* that learners appear to be learning. Review this and look for overriding patterns. Where they exist, point this out to the learner and explore alternative methods.

For every situation that the learner describes as important or significant, ask him/her to reflect on the meaning of the situation as he/she sees it.

At the completion of a learning plan or when difficulties are arising, spend quality time drawing conclusions about the information you have both gathered.

Suggest that the learner shares conclusions with other set members in order to receive different feedback, or validate your conclusions.

What is a Counsellor?

Some people differentiate the role of counsellor from that of coach, as indeed is indicated by including counsellor as one of the roles of the mentor. The proposition generally is that a counsellor as helper is assisting someone to review either longer term career goals, or issues of great personal sensitivity, either about an individual's life in general, or about some worrying aspect of personal behaviour at work. Some managers operate in this role because they are asked to, because they are good at it and because they feel good in doing it. Others would never be invited to be helpful in this area, and others again would certainly never offer themselves for this role. The distinction between helpful discussions centred on performance improvement, and helpful discussion centred on personal growth and development is often difficult to make in advance, and certainly difficult to operate in practice.

The Manager in the Development System

Most of the management development literature is in fact concentrated on this role – the manager as appraiser or reviewer of performance, the manager as contributor to discussions on potential, the manager as contributor to decisions on succession plans. These aspects are reviewed in detail in Chapter 9. Informal opportunities for help must be linked with and supported by the formal management development system. There is no sense in asking a manager to be more helpful in identifying and using opportunities for learning through the job in the informal context, if all the formal system recognizes is appraisal and sending people on courses. Indeed one can turn the point round the other way. For a manager to be helpful on many of the things discussed in this book, there may be a need to challenge what the existing management development system provides to the helping manager. If the system on paper requires the helping manager to sit down and review ongoing learning opportunities, has it also provided the potentially helping manager with training necessary in order to achieve this?

Given that the role of the manager is expressed at its widest, most formidable and most testing currently within the formal management

Chart 7.9   Roles of a manager in developing subordinates

Within Formal System of Development
Appraisal of performance
Appraisal of potential
Analysis of development needs and goals
Recognising opportunities
Facilitating those opportunities
Giving learning a priority
Selecting opportunities in tune with learning styles

Within the Direct Managerial Context
Using management activities as learning
Establishing learning goals
Accepting risks in subordinate performance
Monitoring learning achievement
Providing feedback on performance
Acting as a model of managerial behaviour
Acting as a model of learning behaviour
Using Learning Styles and Learning Cycle
Offering help
Direct coaching
Looking for deputizing/delegation opportunities

development system, the main elements of it can be set out as in Chart 7.9. Most formal systems currently give emphasis to the first three, and insufficient emphasis to the last four on the 'Formal' list.

To Make a Sale, You Need a Buyer

The theme of this chapter is what a helper can provide for an individual, moderated by what the individual is likely to accept. At this stage it is sensible to return to the individual being helped in order further to assist the helper identify what might be helpful.

EXERCISE 7.6   AN INDIVIDUAL'S INTEREST IN BEING HELPED

Imagine that the individual in Exercise 7.2 is the person to whom you might offer help. Consider the following questions, and answer them as best you can as you believe that individual would respond to them.

1. Why am I interested in being helped?
2. Is my interest expressed through informal, normal day-to-day activities and relationships, or because of an opportunity through a formal management development scheme?
3. Which individuals would I consider as potentially helping me through ongoing problems, as mentor or as coach?
4. What are the characteristics I would be looking for which would help create a helpful relationship? What are my previous experiences with the alternative individuals, and how does this indicate what the helping relationship might be like?
5. What kind of situations/activities/tasks do I envisage where help might be needed?
6. What sort of learning opportunities can I recognize?
7. What criteria for success would I suggest as a result of our relationship?
8. What kind of review process would I propose?

The helping manager could now sensibly repeat that exercise, in a role playing exercise with a prospective learner. This time the helping manager could carry it out as a direct personal exercise, i.e. how would I like someone to help me!

What Causes Things to go Wrong?

The case advanced throughout this book has been that opportunities for learning are under-utilized – so that is obviously one of the areas in which the helping relationship can initially go wrong. The helping manager may identify the wrong needs, fail to recognize learning opportunities and fail to provide enough time to review them. Apart from this, there is a useful checklist which any potential helper can use (Chart 7.10).

Chart 7.10   Reasons why helpers fail to help

1. Failure to recognize opportunities for helping an individual to learn
2. Failure to recognize the specific needs of an individual
3. Failure to agree what is being attempted (the Learning Contract in the formal sense)
4. Inability to use a style appropriate to the learner
5. Inability to adapt to implicit or explicit expectations of an open dialogue
6. Inability to adjust power relationships – 'I am the boss, you are the learner'
7. Conflicts on expectations and offers of help between mentors, coaches and learners – and bosses
8. Lack of skill in giving and receiving uncomfortable feedback
9. Lack of organizational support, e.g. from boss, from reward system
10. 'I meant to try, but I have never found the time.'
11. Insufficient or inappropriate development as helper

Developing the Helper

A number of organizations are now running courses on coaching, and a few are running events for mentors. The assumption by many managers that they are coaching, mentoring or helping through problem solving is correct for many of them, but at a much lower level of achievement than is desirable. One of the benefits of going through the exercises included in this chapter will be that individuals are more likely to recognize that there is more to helping someone else to learn than simply being well-intentioned. The development of these skills can be secured by any or several of the following:

- Going on a course/workshop which gives opportunities for identifying and practising the skills involved
- Finding a colleague whose skills you admire, observing, reflecting and discussing those skills with that individual, and experimenting with your own behaviour
- Observing and giving feedback to anyone who is trying to help you
- Observing yourself in action with someone you are trying to help.

Illustrations of the kinds of things which can be done in formal training are given in Further Reading.

Coaching and Mentoring for Qualification

The process required by the Institution of Mechanical Engineers mentioned on page 104 includes the role of mentor as assessor. While no doubt appropriate for the particular circumstances of that kind of professional qualification, it is a role probably not appropriate in the managerial area. What will increasingly occur in the managerial world, however, is that as the structure of national qualifications for managers becomes established there will be a greater demand for more senior managers to act as coaches and mentors. In itself this will lead to a number of very desirable results. It will highlight the role and the opportunities and will no doubt lead to further effort, certainly for those pursuing qualifications. A ripple effect may cause more coaching and mentoring for people not pursuing qualifications who may request similar attention. The only reservation is that the process might be seen by both helpers and learners as so dedicated to the educational qualificational objective as to be primarily an academic and unreal exercise.

Evaluation

Throughout this book it has been emphasized that development ought to be envisaged as a managerial process subject to the same disciplines and controls as other management processes. An important issue for all individuals who want to help others therefore is to evaluate the success of what has been attempted.

EXERCISE 7.7   EVALUATING THE HELP I HAVE OFFERED

1. What was I trying to achieve as the helper?
2. What was the individual trying to achieve as the learner?
3. What did I achieve?
4. What did the learner achieve?
5. What did I learn from the process of trying to help?
6. What are the suggested actions for the next time I try to help an individual?

Chart 7.11   The continuum of behaviour for the developer

Style	When Appropriate
Tell/Instruct	The requirement of the learner is to acquire information and has no problem in accepting it.
Sell/Suggest	The learner is prepared to be led towards a solution to a problem, but not to be told.
Ask/Question	The learner needs to learn the right questions to ask as well as the answers. The situation is not necessarily clear to the developer.
Listen/Respond	The learner is prepared to present the issue/problem but is not necessarily looking for a solution from the developer.

The Continuum of Help

No single style of help is going to suit all situations and all individuals or all helpers. The range of choice is illustrated in Chart 7.11. As indicated earlier, much of the existing material on coaching emphasizes listen/respond. Effective help depends on choosing the right style to match the issue, the situation and the individual being helped.

The Level of Help

One way of looking at help is to define it as being either incremental or transforming. In one case you are primarily attempting to add to and develop existing levels of skills and knowledge. In the second case you may be attempting to move people totally from one kind of managerial world to another, one level of behaviour to a significantly different one, from one level of personal understanding to a much higher plane. For most managerial helpers, the real and present need is usually to facilitate incremental learning. Transformational learning is far more difficult to achieve, requires much more attention than most line managers are likely to offer. In this book the attention is primarily directed at incremental learning. Managers interested in offering a greater transformational challenge will find some useful ideas in books referred to under Further Reading.

Self-development

The purpose of helping is to enable another individual to learn, not to provide yourself with an opportunity to teach. The helper has a major role to play, but the role is to facilitate self-development by the individual being helped.

The Principle of Reciprocity Applies

In helping someone else to develop, the helper is also learning. Not only are the kind of exchanges described in this chapter clearly at their best facilitative of communication and understanding between the two individuals, they are also developmental for the helper in the sense that the skills of the developer can and should improve as their experience of helping grows. However, this learning and development will only happen if the helper carries through the same kind of process of setting objectives, reviewing learning opportunities and reviewing achieved learning in relation to the skill of helping. As a manager said, 'In helping others I am helping myself. I have learned about team performance. I have fewer problems coming across my desk. I have a greater understanding of myself as well as of the individuals who work for me. Best of all, I think I am being more helpful now than I was able to be two years ago.' An effective helping relationship builds on the strengths of the two participants, to create the equivalent of two and a half managers.

How do I Find the Time?

Three reasons were suggested earlier in this chapter why managers engage in the development of others (see Exercise 7.1 on page 98). The big obstacle to spending time in developing others is the lack of immediate return compared with the immediate expenditure of the manager's prime resource – time. Managers are usually very busy people, with many competing claims on their time. The frequency of the problem is attested in one way by the popularity of books on managing time, and also (paradoxically since they consume work time) courses.

An unwillingness to spend time on developing others may only be a particular example of the general problem of the over-committed manager, to which a substantial analysis and action plan might be the best answer. Perhaps the recognition that 'developing others' is one of several desirable managerial priorities not being met might stimulate such an analysis.

An alternative, which deals initially with the specific need to find some time for development, is:

- Look at your diary for this week or last week.
- Assess for each day how much time you now think was used unproductively, e.g. late start to meetings, looking for papers, repetitious discussions, clearing up someone else's problem.
- Calculate your average wasted time.
- Decide which aspects of the wasted time are within your control (most managers can find 30 minutes per day).
- Decide the action you will take to eliminate some of the wasted time.
- Allocate 50 per cent of the time you will save *in advance* to some aspect of helping others to develop.
- Write down the benefit which will accrue to *you* if spend this time developing someone else.

One More Time . . .

The most obvious help managers give others is the provision of opportunities to learn. All too often this is only Big O. The real benefits the manager developer can offer will often arise from encouraging the process of learning review. The following exercise illustrates the point.

EXERCISE 7.8   WHAT HAVE I LEARNED FROM BEING A HELPER?

Look back at a recent experience of helping someone else at work. What have you learned:

1. About yourself?
2. About the individual you have helped?

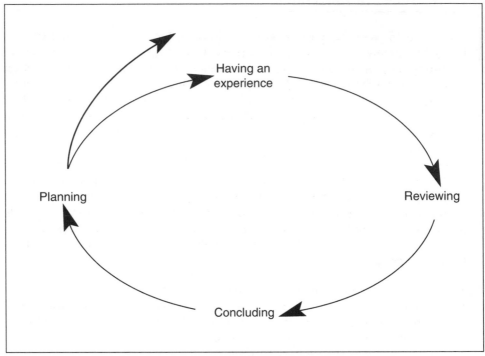

Figure 7.1   The Progressive Learning Cycle

3.   About the process of helping?
4.   About what to do next time?
5.   About the process of reviewing what you have learned?

The Manager Developer Manages

Effective manager developers carry out the helping role by following and giving appropriate attention to each stage of the Task and Learning Cycles. In doing so they are managing the process of helping. They are also learning about the process of managing helping. They are then involved in a more continuous learning process. The Progressive Learning Cycle, introduced in Chapter 4, is shown again in Figure 7.1. The arrow flying out of the original cycle indicates the possibility of a new cycle, or revisiting some stage of the original cycle, e.g. 'I need more information.' 'I did not really sort out my conclusions.'

Case Study 3

It is more than twenty years since I worked for the boss who did most to develop me, Don Stradling. I have an even clearer understanding now of why he was a good manager developer:

- he set clear stretching obtainable objectives for my work
- he provided opportunities to experiment with new ideas
- he passed to me some work he enjoyed doing, instead of holding on to it
- he gave me time to discuss my own work, and his problems too
- he gave me balanced feedback on my strengths and weaknesses
- he provided a range of development options.

EXERCISE 7.9

1. Who has been most influential in your own development?
2. What skills or characteristics did he or she show?
3. What lessons are there for you in this analysis?

8

Learning in groups

The impact of the environment in which the learner works, variously expressed as the culture or the climate – the organization as a mechanism for learning – was discussed in Chapter 5. Powerful though the organization as a whole is in its impact on the individual, the most potent expression of influence comes from the particular actions of other individuals. The organization is a convenient expression for the perceived totality of powerful influences. This chapter concentrates on influencing something larger than the individual, and smaller than the organization – the group.

The intention here is to look at how line managers can help their subordinates or colleagues to learn in groups. The role of the boss is considered here, since it has been argued throughout this book that that is the person with the clearest responsibility and accountability for helping others. In addition, the role of colleagues in the group is of importance, particularly the effect of their activities on whether and how colleagues learn within the group.

The Manager as a Socialized Worker

Amongst the defining characteristics of managers, as compared with senior researchers or professionals, is that they achieve their goals in part through their direct responsibility for the work of others. Of course, a large part of this book expresses that responsibility and accountability in terms of the kind of help which managers should be offering to others. Another aspect of that characteristic is that managers work in and through a variety of groups, some temporary and some relatively permanent. Managers spend relatively little of their time on their own, working mainly in a variety of social interactions. The effectiveness of those interactions is itself a subject for learning by individuals and, of course, by the group as a whole. This is usually described as the 'process' aspect of a working group – the extent to which it facilitates achievement of its objectives and goals through the management of the group dynamic.

Most managers see the purpose of a working group as being primarily the achievement of managerial tasks – the facilitation of achievement by either individuals or the group as a whole of larger-scale or intertwined objectives.

Generally groups spend very little time on process issues unless they have been introduced to some discipline for doing so by attending a course, or by interventions through a process consultant at work. It is even more rare for groups to consider their effectiveness as vehicles for learning. Whereas there is material on how bosses, mentors and coaches can assist individual development, there is much less evidence available on how groups can be made into more effective learning vehicles at work. The final two words are important because the emphasis of this chapter is very much on 'at work'. There is a great deal more available on how effective learning groups can be created off the job through courses, workshops, etc. However, these are designed, constructed and facilitated by trainers and specialist developers, not usually by line managers. For that reason the learning groups constructed in courses are referred to only at the margins in this chapter – just to illustrate areas of knowledge and awareness that a manager might take to a course, or bring back from it. The concern of this chapter is how the line manager helps directly, which predominantly means through real groups or teams at work.

Teams or Groups

It is not the intention in this chapter to summarize all the available knowledge about teams. The aim is just to provide sufficient comment on some of the characteristics of a team at work to provide awareness of some of the issues which are likely to affect the willingness or ability of individuals to learn from the working of the team or group. Once that has been established we can move on the more specific attributes of the learning group or team.

From a managerial point of view there is a significant difference between a collection of individuals brought together in a group, and a collection of individuals brought together as a team. The former is more likely to be temporary, to have no agreed managerial objectives, to have no clear accountability for its performance and often no clear leader. A team, by contrast, is usually more permanent in nature, is accountable for the achievement of defined areas of performance and has a defined leader. A group may have no internal cohesiveness, and may have no real requirement at any level of significance for such cohesiveness. A team may also have no internal cohesiveness in practice, but usually knows that it ought to have in order to achieve its purposes.

For the purposes of this chapter the distinction is not vital. The issues discussed here largely apply whether the collection of people is a group or a team. The significant difference is that because there is a leader of the team – the manager or other person designated to have accountability for its performance – the responsibility for encouraging learning is more obviously centred. The team leader can take the initiative in, for example, describing learning opportunities, encouraging learning reviews and rewarding effective learning behaviours within the team. Within a group, there may be no clear leader and therefore no individual with strong feelings of managerial accountability for encouraging attention to learning. There may of course be a particular individual who wants to concentrate on learning issues, but such an individual will have a harder time than will the leader/manager within a team.

In the rest of this chapter, distinction will be drawn between a team and a group only where it is central to the point being made.

Characteristics of Effective Teams

Precisely because teams can provide ideal situations for the encouragement of effective learning, it is helpful to start with a review of what goes into making an effective team. Not only will the participants recognize first those characteristics which enable them to achieve their managerial objectives, they will also begin to see correlations between those behaviours necessary to managerial achievement and those appropriate to learning. Chart 8.1 is reproduced with permission from Peter Honey.

Some aspects of teams are very familiar to us. They consist of people with all their individual personalities and ways of behaving, but also with managerial functions (e.g. Finance, Production). People bring with them their

Chart 8.1 Characteristics of a good team

- A good team has a high success rate, i.e. more often than not they achieve what they set out to.
- A good team agrees clear, challenging objectives, i.e. everyone in the team contributes to, shares understanding of, and is committed to the objectives.
- A good team has a leader (it may not always be the same person) who adjusts the leadership style along a spectrum from participative to autocratic in the light of circumstances.
- A good team has a mix of people who contribute in different but complementary ways thus achieving synergy, i.e. the team produces more than the sum if its individual parts.
- A good team operates in such a way that a balance is struck between concern for the task (the 'what') and concern for the process (the 'how').
- A good team creates a supportive atmosphere where people are happy to go at risk, say what they really think, develop one another's ideas, commit to an agreed course of action even though there may have been differences of opinion.
- A good team learns from experience, both successes and failures, by reviewing its processes and thus constantly improving its own performance.
- A good team works hard and plays hard, i.e. they not only achieve challenging objectives but enjoy themselves as they do so.

individual personalities and ways of behaving. They bring with them experience, skills and insights into effective management. The team will have disciplines and methods of structuring its work. Group dynamics will involve attitudes and emotions of one person for another, or one sub-set of people for another, which will help or hinder the effective work of the team. It will develop for itself a culture and norms of behaviour.

There are two important characteristics from the learning perspective. The group or team is both a method of learning and an object of learning. It is a way of providing for cross-fertilization of ideas, techniques, problems and solutions. It is also an object of study – 'How does this team achieve its results and what can I learn from that?'.

One of the differences between groups and teams identified earlier is that teams tend to be relatively permanent and groups are often temporary. Within the team the opportunities for learning tend to arise from two different kinds of situation. A departmental management team, for example, will have relatively regular and routine occasions in which it works as a team. Most obviously it will meet together from time to time under the chairmanship of the departmental manager. My research shows that managers learn relatively less from the stable and routine situations and events than they do from the second kind of situation, in which the normal managerial team takes on special responsibilities or a special task. Situations of this kind range from perhaps the annual production of the business plan or budget, through to the investigation of a problem or special decision about some activity, such as 'in view of the decline in sales shall we close down the following three branches?'.

In addition, of course, special teams can be created – task groups, working parties, think tanks, quality circles. These again have the characteristics of teams because they will have an identified purpose, accountability and usually a chairman/leader.

Since we know how powerful teams can be in pursuing shared objectives, the potential for teams to be effective learning vehicles, if they choose to pursue learning objectives as well as task objectives, is considerable. The kind of opportunities available to the team for learning should by now be familiar from earlier chapters in the book. Before reviewing some of these in more detail the following exercise will help to reinforce some of the points made so far.

EXERCISE 8.1

1. Consider groups or teams in which you are currently the leader/manager/chairman/participant.
2. Which do you regard as most effective in achieving its task purpose?
3. Which do you believe is best in terms of managing interrelationships – the process of working?
4. Which do you think is most effective at providing conscious opportunities for learning?

Note that we have started with real teams at work in pursuit of managerial performance objectives. It is within these real teams involved in real managerial work, just as with the individual situations we have reviewed in earlier chapters, that learning within a group starts.

What Sort of Learning?

For a long time one of the familiar ways of describing training was to say that its outputs were knowledge, skills and attitudes. In my most recent research work with my colleagues, Peter Honey and Graham Robinson, we concluded that a more helpful concept than 'attitudes' was 'insights'. A definition of these three words is given in Chart 8.2.

Chart 8.2 Knowledge, Skills and Insights

Knowledge is the acquisition of data or information. Sometimes it is not new knowledge but confirmation of past information.

Skills are the means used to carry out managerial work effectively. The most obvious examples include making decisions, running meetings and negotiating.

Insight or perceptiveness – some people would call it developing wisdom. You can acquire knowledge and skills, but lack the extra dimension provided through insight. Insight is often expressed as conclusions; it helps you generalize from particular experiences.

Examples of Knowledge, Skills and Insight through learning in the group include:

Knowledge	Acquiring information from others in the group, tapping into the expertise of others
	Awareness of the skills and techniques used by others in the group
	Awareness of own skills and techniques
	Awareness of interaction between self and others, and between others
Skills	Personal use of skills of communicating, influencing and listening
	Team use of team skills (see Chart 8.1)
Insight	Awareness of why individuals interact together in the way they do
	Awareness of why the group or team achieves or does not achieve its objectives.

Case Study 1 – The New Manager

A senior manager newly arrived in an organization made a presentation to a management meeting on one of the issues in his department. His arrival in the organization had been greeted with at least polite acceptance and in some cases some warmth by his new colleagues. He was surprised to find that a number of participants in the meeting fell on his proposal as if they were hungry wolves. In reflecting afterwards on what had happened at the meeting and what he had learned from it he identified the following:

Knowledge   He had acquired information during the meeting which had not been available to him in the files he had studied and from people he had spoken to previously. Indeed he had a feeling that some individuals had previously held back information that would have been helpful to him in preparing his proposal. He noted which of his colleagues seemed to him possibly to have been guilty of that, and thought about how he would handle them next time.

Skills   His boss had seen and approved his proposal before it was submitted to the meeting. He admired the way in which she identified a number of positive conclusions arising from the discussion, emphasized the areas in which there was agreement and clarified further action. He admired the way in which she had demonstrated skills in influencing the climate towards a more positive conclusion while at the same time not appearing to attack the criticisms directed at his proposal.

Insights   He concluded that he had not done a good enough political job before the meeting. In his previous organization senior managers were expected to operate through their own initiative and to secure only *concurrence* for any proposal. His insight from this meeting was that in his new organization the expectation was that there would be *consensus* about any proposal from any of the participants, i.e. 'We agree that is what you should do', rather than 'We accept that is what you will do'.

As the example shows, learning within a group consists of:

* learning about yourself
* learning about others
* learning from others
* learning about the group.

Case Study 2 – The Project Review

A team of managers worked for an organization with a single main product. The main product had variations in which individual managers were expert, and which they were keen to sell. As part of the business plan for the year it had been agreed to have a major sales push with prospective and existing clients. This push was intended to form the main priority for all managers, and was called 'Project Multiply'.

Project Multiply appeared as an agenda item for one of the normal team management meetings. Discussions at the meeting revealed that:

- Of the five managers, only two were able to register additional new sales as a result of the project
- There was nonetheless argument about whether the new sales could be attributed to the project, caused by those who had achieved nothing and who apparently wished to denigrate the achievement of their colleagues
- There was no analysis of reasons for success or failure available
- There had been no specific targets set for individuals or for the team as a whole
- Individual members of the team had pursued in some cases the same clients, to offer slightly different products.

The Project Review resulted in a number of decisions, including the identification of targets for individuals, the selection of a prime contact for each client in order to reduce competition between managers, and a commitment to sell the organization's services rather than just those preferred by the individual manager. In addition, the team decided that it would in future require that analytical papers should be prepared and circulated a week before any discussion of items of similar significance. It had learned from its experience that it needed to manage itself better (Experience → Review) had made decisions (Conclude) and agreed what to do in future (Plan Actions) – The complete Learning Cycle.

This case demonstrates not only learning *within* a group, but learning *by* a group.

Learning from Success as well as Failure

Many of the missed opportunities for individuals and for groups to learn occur because there is a greater emphasis on the need to review failure than success. Understandably in view of the pressures and workload for most managers, the tendency is to accept success, sometimes because it is 'normal', sometimes with relief. Failures or partial successes are more likely to be reviewed because it is recognized that something different will need to be done next time. Unfortunately one of the consequences of not spending enough time on reviewing success is that because the causes are insufficiently understood, the superficial reasons for success are applied inappropriately in some subsequent situation – which, of course, leads to failure!

EXERCISE 8.2   REVIEWING SUCCESS AND FAILURE

Look back over the last six months. Consider the following questions:

1. Has your team reviewed, during that time, a significant area of problem, difficulty or failure?
2. What did it learn from this review?
3. Was the learning specific to the particular event, 'This is what we should do if faced with this situation again'? Was the learning more generalized, 'This experience has told us something general about the way in which we operate'?
4. Has your team reviewed a significant success over this time?
5. What did it learn from this review?
6. Was the learning specific to the particular event, 'This is what we should do if faced with this situation again'? Was the learning more generalized, 'This experience has told us something general about the way in which we operate'?

EXERCISE 8.3

Read again Case Study 1 above. This manager was reviewing a failure in his own performance within a group.

1. When you review what he drew from the experience, do you think he learned something specific to presenting a proposal, or something more general?
2. Can you think of similar experiences within your team?
3. What do you believe you learned and what do you believe others may have learned from the experience?
4. What, if anything, have you learned from reading the case study and completing these two exercises?

Balancing Attention to Task and Learning

The last section shows that careful and conscious review of what happens within a team gives the basis for, although it does not guarantee, improved performance in the future. The learning and improvement may, as in the case of the new manager, be primarily individual. Or the learning may, as in the case of the 'Project Review', be very much learning for the team as a whole.

Balancing Task and Learning

In the cases given above, individual and group performance requirements have provided both the occasion and the need for learning. In fact neither the individual nor the group were really aware that they were learning as well as

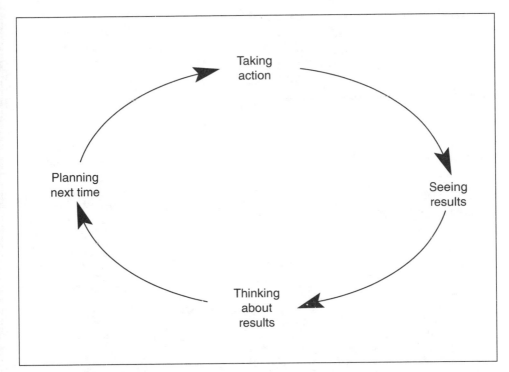

Figure 8.1   Task Cycle

managing until the question was put to them afterwards. They saw themselves as going round a version of the Task Cycle (Figure 8.1). Only after the event were they helped to see that in fact they were also going round the Learning Cycle (Figure 8.2).

Of course it can be argued that achieving the task itself requires that each stage of the Task Cycle be undertaken. Unless the individual manager and the group in the cases mentioned carried out the Reviewing stage, any conclusions about what needs to be done, and any plans about what to do next time, would be likely to be flawed. Effort to take a balanced view of this kind around the Task Cycle in effect also ensures that the Learning Cycle is completed as well. However, the interaction of the two apparently different types of question 'What do we need to do to improve task performance?', 'What have we learned from undertaking this task?', deepens and enhances the quality of the answers for both. The group, asking itself questions about the specifics on the project, was also asking itself questions about what it had learned from the fact that information was missing.

The case for paying close attention to learning is, however, not only that by doing so performance on the task will be improved. Explicit attention to discussion of each stage of the Learning Cycle improves the likelihood of individuals or teams generalizing effectively and appropriately from the particular experience. Note the emphasis on 'effectively and appropriately'.

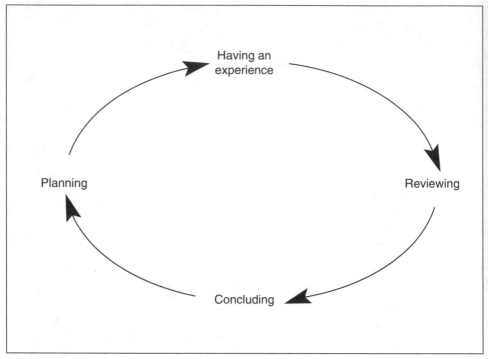

Figure 8.2   Learning Cycle

The issue is not whether managers generalize from particular experiences. This they certainly do. The issue is whether they generalize appropriately and relevantly. My research with managers both as individuals and groups shows that consistently they have learned from experiences at work, but their learning has been inefficient, insufficient and sometimes misdirected. It is only when they have sat down with me after the event – perhaps months or years after the event – that they have fully realized what was involved in an experience, what they learned from it, and sometimes what else they might have learned.

Assisting with Learning in the Group

One of the differences between teams and groups is the presence of a manager accountable for the output of the team. In team situations the responsible manager can provide the most direct help. The absence of a boss in less structured groups means that other people, also often present in teams, will be more evident as helpers. So colleagues, subordinates and clients for services or projects come into play, and in wider groups the grand boss may appear. Sometimes the mentor may make an appearance. Indeed one of the ways in which individuals become mentors informally is through meeting someone in a working group.

The most significant helpers in the team situation are the boss and colleagues.

The boss has to cope with one difficulty which can be inhibiting for learning. While any management discussion can be constrained by the degree to which participants respond to 'what the boss thinks', or 'how the boss behaves', this general issue of expectations and style affects the potential for learning quite specifically. Since learning usually involves asking questions, responding honestly to issues, and taking some personal risks, if these behaviours are inhibited in work situations they will similarly be inhibited when people are asked to discuss openly what they have learned, how they have learned and what they propose to do about their learning.

One of the most useful things a boss can do is to ensure that in the construction of temporary groups or teams attention is given first to the learning process in general. This means establishing for most of them that in addition to their managerial task endeavours they should adopt some learning objectives. 'I want a report on how we should restructure our branch organization. And I also want some comments on what you have learned from working together and generally from the experience of producing the report.' It will be noted that this has been expressed in very brisk, relatively vague, but recognizably managerial terms. This will give readers the general idea of what could be attempted more often with groups.

Of course, it would be possible to be much more sophisticated in setting out learning objectives and including a more substantial learning review. Chart 8.3 shows this.

Chart 8.3 Role of the boss in learning in teams

Puts learning explicitly on the agenda for the team

Identifies learning opportunities arising from managerial work

Sets objectives for learning

Rewards discussion of learning

Suggests criteria for evaluating success of learning

Offers personal statement about own learning

Demonstrates skills of learning

Uses the Task and Learning Cycles as a means of checking the learning process

Identifies and uses individual Learning Styles

Encourages the use of skills of learning

Reviews learning process and achieved learning

Encourages collaborative learning rather than competitive learning behaviour

The last point on Chart 8.3 is worth emphasizing. One of the potential characteristics of groups, and certainly of teams, is that the totality of their analysis and thinking is greater than even brilliant individuals working alone. Synergy rules OK! Recognizing and sharing learning together adds to the learning achieved by each individual.

EXERCISE 8.4   THE BOSS AS ENCOURAGER OF LEARNING IN A TEAM

1.   Consider each item on the chart above and score yourself on a scale 0 = I rarely do this, 10 = I always do this.
2.   Think of a recent team meeting which you managed; how might you have improved your contribution to encouraging learning from it?
3.   Which of the characteristics in the chart do you believe are closest to the way you feel comfortable in operating?
4.   Which are most foreign to you?
5.   Can you select one or more which you might experiment with at a future meeting? Which?
6.   Which meeting?

Case Study 3

A director decided that it would be useful to extend his personal review of learning from experience to his management team. He arranged that each of his regular management meetings should finish with two items:

- 'What have we learned that is important about our business since our last meeting?'
- 'What have we learned today?'

At the first two meetings he gave his own responses first to show he was serious about the process. Subsequently he stood back and let others lead.

Setting Up Temporary Learning Teams

Another important role for the boss is the selection of individuals to work on particular tasks or projects. Normally this will be done by primary attention to considerations of the personal contribution likely to be made by individuals – from their functional knowledge, their experience and their style of contribution. To all these may be added general considerations of 'it would be a good development experience for you'. As described in Chapter 2, this is an example of Big O – the presentation of an opportunity.

A more selective and sophisticated approach can be used by looking at not only the particular learning needs of individuals (see Chapter 9), but also at their learning styles. It is possible to create more effective groups by ensuring that a group has a mix of learning styles.

Case Study 4

In South Africa Mohale Mahanyele, Chief Executive of National Sorghum Breweries, uses the diagnostic results of Margerison and McCann's Team Management Roles, and the Honey/Mumford Learning Styles information as part of the process for constructing project teams. He tries to ensure that there is a distribution of preferred learning styles, so that no group comprises wholly Theorists, or Activists, for example. Chart 8.4 gives ideas on how to use temporary teams for learning.

Chart 8.4 Actions to improve learning in temporary teams

1. Review the information you have on the members. What skills, experience and knowledge do they bring?
2. What do you know about them as learners? Is there a development purpose in their participation? Do you know their Learning Styles/Team Role preferences?
3. What sort of opportunities for learning do you anticipate:

   - from the team's work
   - about the way the team worked?

4. Can you agree a process for discussing learning?
5. Which members are most likely to help in what way?

Learning Skills in a Group

The general argument on the similarity between the Task Cycle and the Learning Cycle and specifically on the stages involved can be extended to the similarity between skills usually identified as being managerial, and skills particularly appropriate to learning. With a few exceptions the skills required for learning are those which managers require for other managerial activities anyway. This is indicated in Chart 8.5, which suggests the kind of skills necessary for effective learning in a group or team. The skills are not only required by individuals, but required for effective development and understanding of learning within the group. For synergy to be achieved, these skills have to be employed. To be employed they need to be encouraged. Chart 8.6 spells out some ways of achieving this.

As shown earlier, while it is certainly the role of the boss to provide encouragement, it is also the responsibility of other members in the team. In looking at skills of learning in the group, we are also looking at how colleagues help the development of others. Discussion earlier in this chapter of collaboration rather than competition has made part of the point. One of the reasons why temporary groups on training courses can be more effective as learning groups than similar groups at work is that competition is reduced although never entirely eliminated. If a team sets itself an objective to be an effective learning team, it needs each individual to take a collaborative stance

Chart 8.5 Individual behaviours in effective learning groups

- Enabling fellows to share air time appropriately
- Non-defensive about own actions and learning
- Supportive about issues/concerns of others
- Open in initiating and responding to issues
- Analytical
- Questioning in style eliciting information not defensiveness
- Listening effectively
- Accepts help
- Creative in response to problems
- Innovative in recognizing learning from task
- Risk taking
- Use Task and Learning Cycles
- Understand and use Learning Styles
- Use strengths of others as learners
- Help motivate others as learners

Chart 8.6 Assessing learning skills in a group or team

1. The members review the strengths and weaknesses of the team or group as a learning unit.
2. Members decide the actions necessary

   - to make effective use of strengths
   - to reduce any weaknesses.

3. Members decide which individuals will have particular responsibilities for their actions.
4. Members decide on a process for monitoring effectiveness in carrying out the actions.

with each colleague in the team, at least as far as learning experiences are concerned. It needs to encourage the constructive use of differences instead of the destructive acceptance of conflict. Most of us have had experience of good and bad teams, and will probably agree that one of the distinguishing characteristics is precisely the greater emphasis on collaboration – even though individual members may be competitive from time to time on particular issues. Outside management we see the power of collaborative support in endeavours such as Alcoholics Anonymous and Weight Watchers. The support offered through such groups and its effectiveness is a powerful indicator to us of what can be achieved on similarly difficult and often very personal issues in management.

The Action Learning process is, of course, one of the most powerful of group learning opportunities, in which participants (Fellows in Adversity, or as I prefer, Fellows in Opportunity) help each other learn from sharing discussion on real work problems. The demonstration of the power of articulated shared learning objectives and processes is one that should be carried more often than it is back into 'normal' management teams.

EXERCISE 8.5 LEARNING SKILLS IN GROUPS

1. Think about the teams of which you are a member.
2. Identify the one which you believe contains most opportunities for the team to learn with and from each other.
3. Think back to the most recent relevant meeting. How far in general do you think the group as a whole exhibited appropriate learning skills?
4. Assess the group on each of the skills in Chart 8.5. Which of the skills were most frequently evident in the meeting you have reviewed?
5. Which of the skills were most evidently not present?

Group Learning Review

Clearly a significant feature of group learning is the review process. In principle this is established through the Task Cycle and Learning Cycle. The questions that could be put to a group in conducting a learning review are essentially those which are asked of individuals (Chart 8.7).

Chart 8.7 Group learning review

1. What task, process, project or activity are we looking at?
2. What are the main characteristics of it?
3. What information do we have on problems, opportunities, successes and failures around the activity?
4. What conclusions do we draw about what we have learned from reviewing the activity?
5. What actions need to be taken by whom and by when to make our learning productive?

It will be noted that yet again essential to achieved learning is the collection of relevant information – the review stage. One of the major contributing factors to this will be Learning Logs kept by individuals. As discussed in Chapters 4 and 5 not all individuals will be equally good at this, so one of the roles of the leader of the team or chairman of the group is to identify and make use of those individuals who will have kept Learning Logs or their equivalent and may therefore have an extra contribution to make.

Helpers as Learners in Groups

Chapter 7 discussed the skills and insights which manager developers need in order to be effective helpers. The experience of helping is something which can be shared with other helpers. A boss or mentor might choose either to share experiences with another individual, or might do so in a larger group.

EXERCISE 8.6   SHARING EXPERIENCES OF HELPING OTHERS

1.   Are there currently occasions on which I can share experiences with others on the issues discussed in this chapter?
2.   Can I take an initiative myself to establish a process for exchange?
3.   Do I need help from someone else (e.g. my boss, Personnel) in order to do so?
4.   What benefits would I expect for myself?
5.   What benefits would I be able to suggest for others?

Other Issues

The emphasis so far has been substantially on conscious, rational processes for helping learning. However, there are significant factors which are essentially emotional in character. While this chapter has been mainly concerned to show how the process of learning in groups can be managed, because it is seen as simply another example of the management process, this is not the sole issue. Around the more careful, conscious, reflective and analytical processes emotional responses are present. They can be motivating, releasing and energizing – managers whose attitude to life in general, and to learning opportunities in particular, is positive. Perhaps more often there are managers, whose emotions are engaged positively on some occasions or in some situations or on some issues, who are turned off and who present a more negative emotional reaction in other circumstances. There are, of course, issues here well beyond the impact of emotions on learning, on which help and discussion is available in other books. Peter Honey and I have spelled out in our workbook *The Opportunist Learner* how some of the attitudes and emotions issues can be tackled by individuals. One of the useful things a group can do, of course, is to share analyses, for example, through the Learning Diagnostic Questionnaire, and then to engage in developing solutions to problems either for individuals or for the group as a whole (see Further Reading for more details on this).

9

Formal development for individuals

Although all sorts of accidental but useful learning opportunities arise without careful definition of what is required for effective performance in a job, we turn now to formal management development processes. Unfortunately many managers lack recent clarification of what their job is for, what the prime results to be achieved through it are, and how performance is to be measured.

The first contribution of a manager to the development of an individual where there is line management accountability to the development is not 'to discuss development needs'. Nor is it to conduct an individual performance review or an appraisal – nor to draw up a personal development plan or learning contract. All these ought to follow a much more basic step. The first and best help is to ensure that the individual has an appropriate, accurate and workable answer to the following question: 'What am I supposed to do?'.

Example 1

Manager X had been promoted to succeed a boss who after a brief period of illness had taken early retirement. He had been deputizing during the period of illness, but with no formal arrangement or statement. 'I was invited to attend meetings instead of my boss, and people were told to talk to me if they had a problem. I was called in on the Wednesday and asked whether I was willing to take over on the Monday. It was a fair assumption, of course, that I would want the job. Moreover, they had already sorted out all the financial and other issues – a big salary increase, promise of a new car, moving into my boss's office and so on. The director who was talking to me said "Of course, you know the job very well so we don't need to brief you really. Things have been going pretty well, but there are one or two areas which need attention that I am sure you know about. I will talk to you as time goes on about anything that comes up that might be new to you. My door is always open anyway so you just come to me if there is anything you are bothered about".

'I asked if there was a job description, and if there were any particular things he wanted me to concentrate on, at least initially. He said he was sure he had a job description somewhere and he would dig it out for me. He threw out a couple of ideas on things he thought were priorities for my immediate attention – I would have liked to discuss them since they did not strike me as being big issues, but he seemed very pressed for time. At the end of the discussion he told me that he had discussed my promotion with the personnel director, and they had agreed to send me on a management course when I had been in the job for six months.'

Example 2

Manager Y was called in to see his new boss, who had been brought in from a different part of the company to replace the previously unsuccessful incumbent. The new boss told Manager Y that he had been given three clear tasks on appointment. The first and most important was to improve the overall performance of the department, and to take whatever steps were necessary in order to achieve this. One of the necessary steps, it was envisaged, was that he would 'get people to shape up or move out'. Rather more encouragingly, a third objective was to develop the potential of good people in the department who, it was felt, had been held back under the previous regime.

Manager Y had gone along to the interview armed with his job description because he had been warned that the new manager was carrying out a review of what people were trying to do. As the new manager quickly established, the job description had been produced two years earlier during a massive job evaluation exercise. 'That tells me something about the job. What about your specific objectives and priorities – have you got something that tells me what you are trying to achieve over the budget year?' Manager Y replied that the previous boss had not attempted to manage people on this sort of basis. 'Well, I am not going to criticize my predecessor. I will simply say that I don't see how I can get improved performance in the department without people like you actually being clear about what you are supposed to do and my having agreed it. That is the most basic thing about how we are going to manage things around here. Sorting that out will tell me something about which people are going to "shape up". It is also essential for the third objective I have been given – I cannot possibly help develop people properly if we have not agreed together what they are trying to achieve and how good they are in the achievement of it.'

Example 3

Manager Z had been selected from outside the company through a fairly prolonged series of discussions. During those discussions the detail of the job had been set out for her, a job description had been passed over to her and her experience and skills had been carefully reviewed and compared with requirements. On arrival in the company Manager Z was given a carefully prepared one week induction programme. At the end of the week a session had been built into the programme in which she was asked to share with her boss her views on the priorities and problems she thought she would be faced with. Her boss discussed this preliminary analysis and then asked that she return two or three days later with a firmer list produced as a result of this first discussion. He suggested that she follow his language, which was to talk about OPP management, which meant managing by Opportunities, Problems and Priorities.

In all three cases the prime need was to clarify job performance requirements in order to assist effective performance – although in each of the examples quoted it was clear that development needs were also likely to emerge from that process of job clarification. The point is worth emphasizing because, unfortunately, some management development schemes manage to misunderstand or miscommunicate the essential purpose of job clarification. The main reason for clarifying what someone needs to be able to do well in a job is to have those things done well; if the process is sold through a formal management development scheme simply as a requirement in order to establish development needs, it is not surprising that a good many managers are unwilling to contribute much useful thought, or indeed any thought at all, to an exercise they see as a distraction without real return from their managerial priorities.

At which point some managers might be inclined to say they would *only* participate in a job clarification process because it was required for management development purposes. 'My people know perfectly well what is expected of them, without us going to all this trouble of writing things down. I am only doing this because the appraisal form requires me to.' When faced with this sort of argument I use something like the following exercise.

EXERCISE 9.1

1. Have you set out in writing within the last three months the priorities for one of your subordinates?
2. If you have not done so, please write down the six priorities which you believe apply.
3. Ask your subordinate to set down six priorities.
4. Decide what level of agreement you expect there to be – 100 per cent, 75 per cent?
5. Exchange your lists.
6. How far have you agreed on the priorities?

In my experience, managers quite often find there is significant disagreement about the priorities, and consequently they are rather less inclined to claim that 'we both understand what the priorities really are'.

One More Time – The Reality of Management

Clarification of objectives, priorities and desired results leads to a concentration of effort and a greater recognition of what needs to be done well. A manager who does absolutely nothing else in formal development will still have made a large contribution to the development of some subordinates through this first step. Of course, most managers will then want to go on to help with development through steps which logically follow from this job clarification. When both parties are sure about what the essential issues are in the job there are two consequent benefits.

First, it ensures that any development proposals within the formal management development system are built on the reality of the job, not on suppositions about it. Especially it means that individual discussions of this kind will lead to development being centred on the core issues and any specific peculiarities of the job, not through some generalized statements about 'what all marketing managers need' or 'all managers need to have their interpersonal skills improved'.

Secondly, initial discussion of the job, and regular reviews of performance in it, help to highlight those specific opportunities, issues and activities which provide development opportunities.

Once more we see the merit of centring management development, whether formal or informal, on the reality of what managers actually do. Development does not have to be thought of in a separate compartment from the management process itself. Managers are more attracted by activities which bring direct managerial results. They give lower priority to activities specifically aimed at learning and development. To suggest therefore that they start from job clarification, from which they and their subordinates will gain immediate managerial returns, is to work with, rather than against, their fundamental concerns.

Delegating and Deputizing

These headings represent both opportunities and traps. An opportunity 'to see what X can do' is a trap if it only involves vague and unclear 'passing down' without clear responsibility, authority and accountability. The main reason for clarity is that without it the managerial task is likely to be carried out inefficiently and ineffectively. From the development perspective, the additional requirement is that learning opportunities are specified and achievement monitored. Indeed, it is setting out these issues that can show up the lack of clarity in the managerial as well as the learning objectives.

Development for What?

When an individual has been helped to establish the main content of the job to be done, there is still one more step before development needs can be established. As just explained, it is fundamentally helpful to know that, for example, one of the priorities to be followed over the next six months is to improve quality, or to develop a closer relationship with the sales department, or to participate in a review of who the customers for your service are. Although the benefits of undertaking precisely this kind of task have been explained initially as directed at improving management itself, in the context of this book we now move to the use of job descriptions, or the OPP (Opportunities, Problems, Priorities) approach to produce development needs.

At one level, these job requirements can immediately produce statements of development, need and opportunity. So, for example, they often lead to the kind of Big O approach mentioned earlier. Therefore, a priority to get close to the customer can be expressed also as a development opportunity – 'you will find out much more about how the customer ticks, and learn something about how to approach people like this in future'.

As already explained, the Big O approach suffers from being too generalized. Useful as a starting point, if left simply as a large scale opportunity it does not produce the most effective learning. In order to become a managed learning opportunity, the specifics of what is involved need to be identified. Following the same example, the learning opportunity involved in 'getting close to the customer', could be broken down into:

- observing how the customer puts over what the organization wants
- observing how your colleagues respond to the customer
- observing the balance between quality, speed of delivery and cost as identified by the customer
- reviewing the presentation skills of the customer, and of your colleagues
- improving your understanding of how things seem from the customer's point of view, as compared with your organization's point of view.

The analysis of large-scale opportunities as the identification of clearer, but smaller, opportunities within Big O, is a process which has not so far been properly taken on within most formal management development schemes. For the reasons indicated earlier, many management development advisers have not yet fully realized the kind of involvement they need to have in order to advise managers on how to make use of such opportunities more effectively.

The more familiar process adopted by most management development advisers, and which therefore many managers will already have encountered, is a process of formally analysing training or development needs either through a breakdown of a job description, objectives or priorities, or through a separate process actually called 'analysing training needs'. This latter term is itself unhelpful and inaccurate. We should, of course, be talking about 'learning and development needs', not training. Training is an input not an output, and in any event carries with it connotations of formal instruction through courses, rather than the totality of the learning world which we ought to be encouraging. Despite the misnomer it is helpful to think of breaking down the large scale statements about what managers do into more concrete, more specific statements of particular kinds of skill or knowledge input. What is it that a manager has to do well? What are the knowledge requirements for effective performance?

The vocabulary of formal management development has over the last ten years been extended beyond the once familiar skills, knowledge and attitude requirements to embrace a newer term, 'competence'. Managers will encounter whatever their own organization has decided the appropriate vocabulary to be. They will be asked to assess the current level of skills, knowledge, attitude or competence.

It is not appropriate in this book to review the arguments for and against the identification of needs through skills, knowledge and attitude as compared with doing so through competences. The competency approach has certainly gripped many formal parts of the management qualification system in the United Kingdom, and seems likely to do so in Australia. The work in these countries largely derives from earlier work in the United States, by Richard Boyatzis. The practising manager is unlikely to want to go into the details of why one approach is better than another, why one set of general competences is favoured over another.

Anyone who wants to delve further into this can do so through the Further Reading on pages 211–13. At this point in our discussion all that is really necessary is to encourage managers to undertake some form of analysis of needs with any individual for whom they have a development responsibility. Whether they use a blank sheet and simply try to devise their own list of skills or competences, whether they use an organization-specific list, or whether they depend on some national competence statement such as that produced by the Management Charter Initiative in the UK, is a matter which will be determined by what is available within their own organization.

As Chapter 1 shows, my own preference is that managers work, whenever possible, to an organization specific list rather than accepting too readily a national competence list. For that reason I give in Chart 9.1 an example from one organization, rather than the MCI.

Chart 9.1 is taken from *Managing Careers* by Andrew Mayo and reproduced with permission of the publishers, The Institute of Personnel Management, IPM House, Camp Road, Wimbledon, London SW19 4UX.

Development for Now, or the Future?

The steps established so far will be helpful in establishing what the job is now, and what the skills or competences required to do it effectively are. Of

Chart 9.1 Skills and experience for general management in the 1990s International Computers Limited

Experience

E1 Line management accountability for specific deliverables relating to the business results.

E2 Significant P&L financial accountability.

E3 Significant man management accountability through at least two levels of subordinate management.

E4 Commercial experience – personal involvement in customer or supply negotiations.

E5 International experience – preferably through physically working outside the home country or extensive involvement in working with overseas countries.

E6 Staff appointment – responsible for helping influence line managers to perform better in a particular function of their role.

E7 Has operated within more than one division in this organization or in other companies.

Skills

S1 A good team leader, able to weld together and use complementary knowledge and skills towards common objectives.

S2 A good strong people-manager, fair/firm, balancing task/team/individual needs, known for developing staff.

S3 Able to delegate accountability.

S4 A strategic thinker – demonstrates wisdom, sees the overall company as well as local need, formulates tactics within an articulated strategy.

S5 One who sees and seizes opportunities within agreed strategies.

S6 Able to multiprogramme a large number of issues at any given time, and keep all major accountabilities in progress.

S7 Able to balance long-term requirements against short-term objectives.

S8 Able to manage conflict constructively, with peers or peer groups.

S9 Able to adapt management style to different needs.

S10 Skilled at communication, especially verbally.

S11 A good probing relevant questioner, and a good listener.

S12 Ready to take necessary decisions at the right time.

S13 Able to cope with stress without loss of performance.

S14 A controlled risk taker.

S15 Has a personal presence that can command respect internally and externally.

S16 Personal ambition – desire and drive to take senior accountability.

course, people can be developed for a different job – usually one involving promotion. In considering this we enter an even more difficult arena. The process of job clarification and identification of skills or competences is problematical enough for most managers. To move from that to establishing development needs, though a logical step, is also one which sometimes is found difficult – it is easier to say that someone needs to be better at his or her job than it is to break that statement down into usable propositions. To move from that into identifying development needs for a future job is additionally difficult.

The attempt to combine appraisal of present performance and identification of potential is fraught with difficulty. The basic problem is one of moving from the actual, i.e. performance in the current job and development needs arising from that performance, to the hypothetical situation of someone occupying a different job in the future. Some skills and knowledge will be brought to that job from the existing one, but they may be required at a higher level of intensity or a deeper level of skill or knowledge. Other aspects of a new job may involve quite different skills or areas of knowledge.

It may be possible to identify these fairly clearly. If you are moving someone, for example, from a sales job into a marketing job, it ought to be possible to take the content of the prospective new job and the kind of skills involved in it and relate those to the skills currently possessed by the person you are moving from sales into marketing. Unfortunately, though understandably, many line managers are too impatient and insufficiently committed anyway to undertake such a neat analytical and logical process. They tend to revert rather readily to statements such as 'he will need to be broadened in skills and experience in order to undertake the potential new job'. Since this book is written for those managers who are prepared to devote some time and energy to these considerations, some of the steps which should be undertaken are set out in Chart 9.2.

Chart 9.2 Developing an individual for promotion

- Review with the individual what her or his career plan or ambitions are.
- Discuss how realistic these ambitions are and how they may be attained within the existing organization.
- Discuss the differences between a prospective job or jobs and the one currently held by the person with whom you are involved.
- Discuss the levels of skills, knowledge, experience and competence required in the new job as compared with what your interviewee currently has.

My experience agrees with research, which has shown that the identification of potential amongst individuals is a highly suspect operation. This is partly because insufficient effort is devoted to the steps indicated earlier, i.e. definitions of what is required in a new job, and also the familiar problems of actually establishing what the real level of performance by a job holder is currently. It is therefore understandable and indeed almost legitimate for organizations to throw a lot of development opportunities at people somehow identified as having high potential, in the hope that those who turn out to have been properly identified, i.e. those who succeed to higher jobs, will have been through appropriate development experiences. To give large numbers of people development opportunities which may help them in the quest for jobs of a different kind or at a senior level also helps to satisfy the uneasiness increasingly felt about too meritocratic an approach within organizations. Not only is the meritocratic approach seen as having failed in its accuracy of prediction, but there is a feeling that it closes down and restricts opportunities in a way which is not only inefficient, but also perhaps in some sense immoral.

The basis of this argument has been misguided. Because of the emphasis on providing relatively expensive courses, decisions about which priorities, and therefore about which individuals, should be exposed to programmes of development for the future are in my view necessarily organizational realities. If, however, the view of development taken is the one suggested in this book, namely one which is centred very much on real work opportunities, there is much less reason or need to limit them from developing greater potential. For every important decision about sending someone expensively to Harvard, there are many smaller opportunities available for larger numbers of people to work on projects, task groups and similar assignments. Decisions on this need not be so restrictive.

When to Diagnose Development Needs

Many existing management development schemes provide a simple answer to this issue. Needs are diagnosed once a year through an appraisal, performance review or development review process set up as a major feature of the management development system. Desirable though this is as a means of catching the attention of busy managers at least once a year, this has the problem that it emphasizes the extent to which diagnosing development needs happens only once a year and at a prescribed time. While certainly better than not doing anything at all, the problem is that in the turbulent, constantly changing world which is managerial reality development needs do not neatly occur once a year, nor do they, once identified, necessarily remain relevant and accurate for a year. While not abandoning the once-a-year review which has the merit of ensuring that something happens, managers need to provide help when help is needed.

The three examples at the beginning of this chapter indicate the kind of circumstances which occur quite frequently. Two of the examples centre on someone moving into a new job, the third revolves around a change in the environment – a new boss with quite different ideas (and indeed the specific task of producing development plans).

In summary then, development needs need to be assessed:

- on those regular occasions prescribed by a management development system;
- on those occasions when an individual changes job;
- when there is a major change in the working environment for the individual.

Recognition of and action on these latter occasions would be a major advance in many management development systems. Again in managerial reality they contain the extra persuasive ingredient. Development needs can be assessed in changing circumstances precisely because the circumstances make the need clear, as compared with the management development system which may often seem to be an external and relatively routine imposition.

Just as the once-a-year review, though helpful, is of limited value because of changes during the year, so diagnosing needs on the occasion of a particular job change or environmental change contains a similar problem – it provides an answer relevant to the immediate time but not necessarily over a longer period. A person going into a new job in fact goes through different stages of learning requirement. John Gabarro's excellent research suggests the following stages in Chart 9.3 when a manager enters a new job, each of them containing different learning needs and opportunities.

Chart 9.3   Stages in taking charge (Gabarro)

1. Taking Hold
2. Immersion
3. Reshaping
4. Consolidation
5. Refinement

We have touched on a number of the circumstances in which change of job or environment can stimulate development needs. Chart 9.4 sets out a range of possible changes.

Chart 9.4   Changes in job or environment

Change in Job – *Same Function*

* To new organization
* Within same organization but different section
* Within existing section but different job.

Change in Job – *Promotion*

* To new organization
* Within same organization but different section
* Within existing section.

Change in Job Content – *Additional Responsibilities*

* Acquiring new responsibilities within existing job
* Appointment to Committee/Task Force/Project Group.

Change in Job – *Secondment*

* Move to another organization
* Move within same organization.

Change in Environment

* New boss
* New objectives/priorities
* New organization structure
* New customer
* New standards of performance.

There are two ways of testing the meaning of this section. Readers can review the circumstances described in terms of what has happened to them over, say, the last two years. Secondly, they can assess how far the circumstances apply to people who now work for them. The following exercises provide for this.

EXERCISE 9.2 CIRCUMSTANCES CREATING DEVELOPMENT NEEDS FOR YOURSELF

1. Review the circumstances described in Chart 9.4; which of them have applied to you over the last two years?
2. Did you recognize that there were learning and development needs arising from these changed circumstances?
3. Were you assisted in this recognition by, e.g. your manager or someone else?
4. What action did you or anyone else take to assist with your learning or development needs?

EXERCISE 9.3 CIRCUMSTANCES CREATING DEVELOPMENT NEEDS FOR OTHERS

1. Review the list given in Chart 9.4.
2. Have there been changes of this kind which have affected people who now work for you?
3. Did you recognize, and did you help them to recognize, that learning needs arose or would arise from these changes?
4. What help did you provide to the individuals?

Diagnosing the Content of Development Needs

If a manager has gone through some process of job clarification, of skills or competence identification, then the content of development need will begin to emerge. The needs will either be prospective, i.e. things which you think someone is going to need because of changes in the job or environment, or they will be retrospective, i.e. they will be identified from the current performance in the job. A third category is development needs not required in the current job but required, as indicated earlier in this chapter, in advance of movement to a different or more senior job. This can be simply set out as follows:

*   Development needs arising from current performance
*   Development needs forecast for this job
*   Development needs presumed for another job.

Another way of looking at the kind of development needs which emerge is centred on the idea of 'ownership' of needs. While the manager as helper may have a very clear view about what someone else needs, the other person may not only lack clarity about the needs, but could also lack commitment. We will look at this latter issue in more depth in the next section. At this point we raise some points about the content of development needs different from the time related issues just discussed. Both the helping manager and the person being helped may identify a large number of development needs. As a useful check on any tendency towards an over-enthusiastic collection of too many needs, the scales in Chart 9.5 are helpful.

Chart 9.5   Scales of importance for development needs

Desirable	→	Crucial
Interesting	→	Usable
Valuable in general	→	Specifically relevant
Action some time	→	Action now
Important for this job	→	Important for future job
Specific for this individual	→	Generally useful for managers

Again it will be helpful to assess the usefulness of Chart 9.5 through the following exercise.

EXERCISE 9.4   IMPORTANCE OF DEVELOPMENT NEEDS

1. Consider the development needs of someone who works for you. (You may have material from an appraisal, a recent discussion, a particular occasion where needs have been revealed.)
2. Use Chart 9.5 to assess or re-assess the priorities you have given to the development needs of the individual, first for the current job, then for a future job.
3. What conclusions do you draw from this review? Have you changed your view about priorities? Have you found that you have identified too many needs?
4. What was the balance between the ideas for development you put into the plan, and those contributed by the other individual?

How to Diagnose Development Needs

The prime requirement is to base the process of diagnosis on what managers actually do. This can be assessed through the steps of job clarification, skills or competence analysis and the use of precipitating managerial circumstance described earlier. Many organizations now provide not only a formal system of appraisal, performance review, potential review and personal development planning, but also provide guidance on how to conduct an appraisal effectively, and probably provide guide books giving helpful hints both to appraiser and appraisee. These are, of course, contributors to identifying and meeting development needs. Since there is so much guidance available both in text books and in organizational material on these subjects, and since the particulars obviously vary between organizations, it is not proposed to add to those 'How To' statements here. (See Further Reading for material if required.) There are a few statements which will be helpful in the development perspective of this book.

There is an inevitable tension between the hard edge of reviewing performance, and the apparently softer management issue of development needs. On the one hand development needs must be centred on carefully identified performance issues. However, the process of identification, if not carried out sensitively, may destroy the willingness of the subordinate to accept either the reality of any performance defect or the relevance of any development need or solution. That is one of the reasons why some organizations separate appraisal in performance review terms from the production of development plans. There seem to be as many cases of organizations which believe they have secured effective development by clear association with performance review as there are organizations which have separated them with equivalent claims for success.

The second point to be made about both appraisal and performance development plans is that they suffer from defects in implementation. There is a greater willingness to recognize and place on paper needs and solutions than there is apparent capacity to follow through with action. 'Every year we sit down and review my performance. A few weeks later I sign the form that records our discussion. But nothing much happens. I suspect my boss only carries out the appraisal because Personnel nag him if he doesn't.'

Thirdly, as already indicated earlier, any once-a-year process, although essential as a monitoring effort that development is reviewed at least once a year, suffers from the time and context related problem mentioned above. It may miss some important issues and development opportunities.

Fourthly, those schemes and forms which provide for both performance review and the identification of development needs at the same time seem often to provide managers with psychological and information overload. I have experienced the problems of trying to separate them in order to improve attention to development; I found it difficult because managers were often unwilling to devote two sessions rather than one in their busy timetable. The reason for separation is that all too often by the time the participants reach the development needs and solutions section, they are faced with the psychological problem that they have usually dealt with those issues which they regarded as most important, so development very much falls into second place. In addition, time often has become an enemy. 'Is it 5.30 already?'

It seems desirable, therefore, to find a better balance between performance review and development, while still somehow basing development firmly on a review of performance. This can be secured if the appraisal or performance review process takes people as far as identifying development needs, but does not get into solutions and plans. These can be picked up in a second session with a brief revisiting of the performance issues, with reasonable time allocated now to working more specifically on the needs, solutions and drawing up a plan. This is a less clear separation than that adopted by some organizations, which stop at the performance review and take up personal development plans as an entirely distinct process. This does not seem to me the best process. If the arguments about using managerial performance and managerial reality as the basis for development offered in all the chapters so far are accepted, then clear separation is not the right approach. Any process which over-emphasizes the extent to which development is an activity separate from performance will lead to a recurrence of the 'management development is an unreal optional extra' disaster.

The most sophisticated form of performance review is that conducted through assessment centres. These operate largely through simulations of management work providing an opportunity for assessment of individual performance, with supporting data from personality or style questionnaires. The same techniques are often used in development centres, where the objective is to identify development needs rather than assess for selection and promotion. The role of line manager is to assist in creating the skill or competence statements which form the basis of assessment, and to participate in the centre as an observer and assessor. It is precisely because these centres demand so much of the line manager in prior commitment and time that they are difficult and expensive to run, even for large organizations.

Defining Learning Opportunities

The turbulent nature of the managerial world constantly provides both the need for and the opportunities for learning. We have seen a number of them in earlier chapters. An important task for the manager helping others is in the first stage – identifying learning opportunities which can be drawn from particular managerial tasks, activities and circumstances. Of course, a general recognition that opportunities exist or can be created is not enough – that just leads to Big O. What is needed is a discipline for identifying and reviewing learning opportunities. One way of doing this has already been indicated in Chapter 3, in Exercise 3.3 on pages 39–41. Another way is provided in Exercise 9.5 below.

EXERCISE 9.5   PLANNING TO USE LEARNING OPPORTUNITIES

1. Think of one of the people working for you (different from the individual you identified on page 38), whose development is currently in your mind.
2. Review the list of learning opportunities on pages 39–41 and note those which are available and which you are using.

3. Review the list and similarly indicate which opportunities are available but you have not so far used with the individual.
4. What action might you now take to help that individual make use of those opportunities?
5. How would you create the situation in which you might give this advice?

This is a process which can be taken up with individuals at any time, either because the need has emerged from an appraisal or from a personal development discussion or simply because you and the person involved want to think about using learning opportunities more successfully. An even more sophisticated version of this is the creation of circumstances in which learning opportunities are regularly reviewed as an inherent part of a management review system. Once again instead of the management development process being directed as an activity essentially separate from management, we use the management process itself as the occasion for identifying learning opportunities. Charles Handy in an article in *The Director* in June 1992 talked about learning from the incidents in one's life and work. 'It has to be organized, this incidental learning, because the time for it does not come naturally; but it could be that this time for reflection, for incidental review, by individuals with their groups, would do more to improve performance than any number of appraisal interviews.'

Personal Development Plans, Learning Contracts, Learning Agreements

We have established so far the following stages in formal structured development for individuals:

- job clarification
- identification of skills, knowledge, competences, experience required
- assessment of performance against those requirements
- identification of learning opportunities.

The final stage in the process is the production of a plan for meeting development needs. I use the term 'Personal Development Plan' not simply because I have been using it for a long time, but because I think it indicates strongly the three required elements. I also find that many of the managers with whom I deal prefer the term 'Plan' to 'Contract' or 'Agreement', since it is a more generally appropriate managerial word. Certainly a number of them do not like the apparently legalistic connotations of 'Contract'. Some people favour the term 'Learning Agreement' because it clearly implies the two parties to the process. Perhaps the least favoured term is 'Learning Contract', and it is relevant to note that this really emerged from the education system in the United States and was essentially a contract between tutor and trainee. In origin, therefore, the phrase was not really applicable to a process agreed between managers and their people, in a work not an educational context.

The important issue is, of course, what goes into the plan or agreement or contract, and how it is set up. Essentially it is achieved through a process which builds on some version of the steps identified at the beginning of this section – in other words it is built on some view of a gap between performance requirements and performance achievements. For most line managers the performance element is the crucial motivating point. It is not true for other kinds of helpers in the development of people. Counsellors, educators, developers and trainers – the professionals in the management development field – may not only feel no obligation to start there but indeed may feel an antipathy to doing so. For managers, this performance starting point is fundamental.

The first point to make is that the performance requirement statement should never be taken for granted. The fact that an appraisal has been conducted at some time, even relatively recently, is not a reason for avoiding some discussion of performance issues. Nor should a manager simply leap in with a statement such as 'It is probably a good idea if we sit down and work out some plan for your personal development'. Although the Personal Development Plan can indeed be built on a previous session on performance review the start of the discussion should always be to summarize the issues previously discussed. In practice indeed, it may well be that there has been no previous significant performance review discussion. I work a great deal with directors and senior managers, many of whom do not participate in a formal appraisal process. The guidance I give managers in that situation is that discussions between them should follow the sequence in Chart 9.6.

Chart 9.6　Headings for Personal Development Plan

- Main purpose and objectives of current job
- Summary of experience gained on the way to the present job
- List prime issues and problems as perceived by the job holder affecting individual performance
- List contextual factors influencing individual performance
- What are the major items of skill, knowledge or experience required for effective performance in this job?
- What do you regard as your strengths and potential areas requiring improvement?
- What developmental experiences have been significant to you?
- What opportunities for development do you recognize within the current job?
- What career ambitions do you have which could influence future development needs?
- What ideas do you have on solutions to your development needs?
- Do you have any preferences on the way you like to learn?

The list in Chart 9.6 may seem formidable, and indeed can be abbreviated where information is already available which does not need to be discussed again. The reflective analysis can then be followed by the crucial final item:

- What action should be taken by whom and when to ensure development proceeds?

An example of a Personal Development Plan form used by Brooke Bond Foods is shown as Figure 9.1.

The issue of joint involvement in discussion of needs and solutions is fundamental. On something as personal as improving skills and abilities, the chances of needs being successfully identified, let alone met, by a process which does not give full weight to the views of the individual are very low. Individuals are primarily responsible for their own development; the task of the manager is to help with that development, not to attempt to impose views. Of course, the manager, from greater experience, wisdom or knowledge, may have strong views about what the needs are and how they should be met. But help offered in a form, style or tone of voice which is unacceptable to the individual needing development is not help at all, whatever the views of the person delivering it may be.

Solutions to needs must be based on the learning principles discussed in Chapters 4 and 5, so the manager developer must be aware of:

- The need for any personal development plan and for activities within it to follow carefully and in a balanced way using the principles of the Learning Cycle (see page 49).
- The need for solutions to recognize the different preferences for ways of learning individuals may have, expressed in the concept of Learning Styles (see page 53).

In addition to the specific material on Learning Styles available through Honey and Mumford's Learning Styles Questionnaire, or Kolb's Learning Styles Inventory, there are other diagnostic instruments touching on various aspects of personality or managerial style. Amongst the most popular and usable is the Myers, Briggs Types Indicator. The various psychological and personality questionnaires developed by Savill and Holdsworth in the UK or Cattell's famous 16PF widely used in the United States may similarly help with assessing needs, but on the personality rather than the performance dimension.

Example of Personal Development Plan

The following case study illustrates my descriptive approach, which can be contrasted with the brisker style indicated by Figure 9.1.

Case Study: Personal Development Plan

Managerial Experience
His experience has been in Engineering, Production and Project Management.

BROOKE BOND FOODS LIMITED

PERSONAL DETAILS

PERSONAL DEVELOPMENT PLAN

NAME:

DIVISION:

JOB TITLE:

DATE PREPARED:

	DEVELOPMENT OBJECTIVE	DEVELOPMENT ACTIVITY/EXPERIENCE	RESPONSIBILITY	TIMESCALE	RESOURCES REQUIRED
1.					
2.					
3.					
4.					
5.					

Figure 9.1 Personal Development Plan

150

In addition to a variety of offices and works in the UK he has had assignments in South Africa and Denmark.

He is General Manager of a £10 million turnover company, and has held that position for three years.

Personal Experience and Development

He thinks the main areas missing from his experience have been Product Development and Marketing. Although he has not worked in Finance or Human Resources he feels his experience with these has been secured through the jobs he has held so far. Similarly because he was involved in actually selling a number of Project Management jobs, he thinks he has developed a number of the skills in that job.

However, the area he identified as being most important to him at the present time is that of Strategy. He took over a company with a well organized business plan in a context of relatively secure markets. He sees this as a change likely to occur as the environment is going to become much tougher in the next year or so.

Possible Development Needs

Marketing

Product Development

Finance (despite the comments made earlier he recognizes a need for higher level finance knowledge)

Role of a General Manager (he is not always sure of the level of detail at which he should operate, the use of his network within the Group and generally what should be expected of him)

He identified a few areas of skill in which he feels he might be developed:

- Setting clearer targets and objectives for his people
- Selection skills especially interviewing
- Team management dealing with customer problems.

Possible Development Processes

His scores on the Learning Styles Questionnaire indicate that he has a strong preference for the Pragmatist Learning Style, and also Reflector. He has a moderate level on the Theorist and low on the Activist.

Discussion of these preferences showed that they were a correct assessment. He has, for example, been on several courses which he criticizes in retrospect strongly because they seem to have nothing to do with the industry in which he works (Pragmatist). He has also recently turned down an opportunity to go on an Outdoor course, perhaps not surprisingly in terms of his low preference for the Activist dimension.

Activities which might be attractive to him include:

- involvement in some industry wide committees on which he does not currently sit, where he would be exposed to more Marketing and Product Development issues.

- a planned series of discussions with the Group Finance Director and his Divisional Director going over some of the proposed new financial reporting arrangements.
- an Interviewing Skills Course which would not necessarily have to be industry based.
- preferably a substantial visit of two or three days to the Group Business Strategy Department, provided that clear objectives and end results could be defined. This should be preceded by recommended reading.
- The fundamental issue of what his role as General Manager is should be covered by some recommended reading, and some arranged visits to three other General Managers in the Group.

A good way to test the principles of the Personal Development Plan is to try it out. Readers might like to do so through the following exercise.

EXERCISE 9.6   PERSONAL DEVELOPMENT PLAN

1. What have been the main areas of experience you covered on the way to your present job?
2. What do you believe to be your most effective skills?
3. Which of your skills do you believe need development for your current job?
4. What areas of knowledge or experience need to be developed for your current job?
5. What views do you have about possible future jobs in this organization?
6. What skills, knowledge or experience development would you see as desirable for another job?
7. What opportunities for development do you recognize in or around your job?
8. What other development opportunities would you be interested to pursue?
9. What actions can you take, when?
10. What actions should someone else take?
11. How will you measure the results of this plan?

The Management Charter Initiative, Competences and Plans

The idea of using a review of achieved learning, preferably based on a development plan, has been given impetus by the MCI and the associated Managerial Qualifications. The concepts of Accrediting Prior Learning, or Crediting Competence, will certainly give a further push to both creating plans and monitoring achievement. The concept of the Portfolio through which a manager records managerial activities, competences and learning is an excellent development.

Making Effective Use of Courses

While a great deal of the emphasis of this book is on successfully using experiences in and around work as a development tool, undoubtedly courses can be a productive and indeed often uniquely appropriate way of dealing with a development need. Unfortunately it is still the experience of many trainers and educators that people arrive on programmes who have been 'sent', with no significant previous discussion between themselves and their boss. Without such a discussion participants all too often lack motivation, enthusiasm and indeed a basic understanding of why anybody thinks they should attend the course – what needs do they have that the course may help to meet? For what are after all unique investments of time and money a manager developer ought to give assistance. Preferably it will start through the processes we have described so far – if a person has been through a job clarification exercise, understands skill requirements and perhaps some desired areas for improvement and is actually working to an overall development plan, this provides absolutely the best context. Much less success will come from the sudden intervention of a course, to which person is nominated out of the blue with no significant contextual discussion. Chart 9.7 represents a minimum of pre-course discussion between the manager and the person being nominated.

ICL has developed a very positive and detailed approach to this subject as shown in Figure 9.2 reproduced with permission.

The ICL manager is required to sign a Personal Development Plan produced by the subordinate, and then to assess achievement against that plan. If the subordinate has achieved the plan, he or she receives a Certificate.

Chart 9.7 Pre-course discussion between learner and manager

- What areas of personal development is it believed the programme may help me with?
- What information is there about the content, methods and experience of tutors delivering the programme?
- What information is there available within this organization from people who have attended this or similar programmes in the past?
- What specific problems, opportunities and skills do you expect the participant to work on during the programme?
- What help will you as the manager provide before the programme, during it (i.e. leave the participant alone!) and after?
- What arrangements can be made now for a review after the programme of what the participant has learned? What can be suggested for action back in the organization?

MEMORANDUM

STAFF TRAINING

TO **THE MANAGER OF THE DELEGATE**	FROM	R.R.Guy WSR 01
	REF NO	**mfs/5/0-3**
	TEL (ITN)	7269 2441 EXT
	DATE	**Date**

THE ICL MANAGEMENT PROGRAMME
MANAGING FOR SUCCESS

A member of your staff has been nominated for the above management development programme and I am writing to you to explain what is involved, both for the delegate and for yourself. Management training is of course a major investment of time and effort. This briefing pack has been produced to help you to maximise the return on that investment.

KEY ACTIONS YOU MUST CARRY OUT IMMEDIATELY

1. Check the suitability of the programme for your subordinate.The attached INTRODUCTION TO THE PROGRAMME will help you do this.

2. Read the INTRODUCTION TO THE PROGRAMME to familiarise yourself with the style of the programme.

3. Schedule time well in advance of the course to carry out an INITIAL ASSESSMENT OF DELEGATE PERFORMANCE. Discuss this with the delegate in order to clarify the areas to concentrate on most, and to agree development objectives.

4. Ensure that the delegate makes time (about 4-6 hours) to study the pre-course reading.

5. Schedule time in your diary immediately after the course to discuss implementation with the delegate.

YOUR ROLE IN THE MANAGEMENT TRAINING PROCESS

Since the programme is about effective performance in employment, you as the delegate's manager are a key component.

The Management Training Team will provide the delegate with the necessary knowledge, and a suitable opportunity to develop the skills in a safe environment.

Your role is then to provide the opportunity to perform, and to monitor progress towards the award of a certificate. We will provide you with the necessary guidance and support to enable you to do this.

Figure 9.2   The ICL Management Programme

This latter stage deals with one of the weaknesses of plans whose implementation is not monitored.

The Roles of the Helping Manager

In this chapter the primary concern has been to look at the role of the boss as developer of others. The system of management development may also give specific roles to a mentor, or it may ask someone to take on a formal role as coach. As we have already discussed, managers quite often assume the role of mentor but not as part of a formal management development system. There are arguments for and against extending the mentor role into the management development system. The first of these is that by doing so the responsibilities and skills involved become clearer and the need to work on them becomes evident. Issues about the content of the role, the skills involved and how these skills can be developed were covered in Chapter 7.

An overview of the role of a manager in developing subordinates is shown in Chart 9.8. It can be used as shown in Exercise 9.7. The results are salutary in groups of managers who see significant differences. It is illuminating, but needs careful handling, for a boss and subordinate to share their scores.

Chart 9.8   Roles of a manager in developing subordinates

Within formal system of development

- Appraisal of performance
- Appraisal of potential
- Analysis of development needs and goals
- Recognizing opportunities
- Facilitating those opportunities
- Giving learning a priority
- Selecting opportunities in tune with Learning Styles

Within the direct managerial context

- Using management activities as learning
- Establishing learning goals
- Accepting risks in subordinate performance
- Monitoring learning achievement
- Providing feedback on performance
- Acting as a model of managerial behaviour
- Acting as a model of learning behaviour
- Using Learning Styles and Learning Cycle
- Offering help
- Direct coaching
- Looking for deputizing/delegating opportunities

EXERCISE 9.7

1.   Appraise yourself on Chart 9.8 'Roles of a Manager'. On a scale 0 = low, 10 = high, how effective do you think you are?
2.   Where you have a low score, do you need some help yourself in order to improve the help you can give others?
3.   What score would you give your boss on the same chart?
4.   Should you discuss these results (yourself and/or your boss) with someone else?

The Need for Integration

This chapter has indicated a number of aspects of the formal management development system as a defined and identifiable process of 'management development'. However, the emphasis throughout has also been on how to integrate within that formal management development system those features of informal development which are too often ignored by the formal system. The formal management process must embrace, make use of and improve those informal and accidental opportunities which were described in Chapters 1–3.

It will be helpful if readers undertake the following exercise.

EXERCISE 9.8

1.   Consider one of your people for whom a Personal Development Plan might be appropriate.
2.   Use the headings indicated in Exercise 9.6, or develop your own headings for a discussion with such a person.
3.   What information do you have which will assist you in the discussion – appraisal, interview notes, questionnaire information?
4.   What preliminary thoughts do you have on the answers that might be given to the person involved?

10

Formal development for groups

Much the most powerful intervention by a manager in order to help development will be offered through the one-to-one opportunities and activities emphasized in the chapters so far. Whether we look at it from the perspective of the relatively informal and accidental processes of earlier chapters, or the more formal, structured ideas presented in the last chapter, the directness of one-to-one personal interaction clearly provides great opportunities. Because those opportunities are insufficiently recognized and used, and because personal interaction is, by its nature, potentially so productive, that has been the first emphasis in this book.

Ironically, much of traditional formal management development has concentrated instead on working through generalized approaches appropriate, as it was thought, to groups of managers. This has been especially true for those versions of management development called 'Management Training' or 'Management Education'. These have provided a statement of what managers need, and a process or collection of processes thought to be appropriate to meeting those needs. We find courses aimed at managers of all types, or at particular functions, such as marketing or finance, or at one level in an organization – 'this course is appropriate for managers of grades 5 and 6'. We find courses built either around a specific method – the Harvard Case Study, Outdoor or Adventure Training, Action Learning – or designed on the principle of a mixture of activities. Principle is perhaps too grand a word to use for the design of many programmes, which really seem to use a variety of methods – lectures, case studies, videos, business games – more through a concern for variety rather than elegance in design.

Of course, there are needs existing within groups, which can and should be satisfied by generalized approaches through courses, job rotation, secondments and all the other weapons in the armoury of formal management development. In view of the balance of attention in formal management development schemes in the past, however, it is sensible to give a cautionary note first. One of the best things that managers can do in considering how to help others is to decide first how they can help with individual needs, rather than resorting too quickly to the approaches appropriate to meeting needs which might be shared amongst a group of managers. The question should not be 'Can these needs to met through a group solution?', but rather 'Can this need *best* be met through a group solution?'.

Starting from Organizational Needs

One of the areas in which the ability of internal training organizations to meet managerial development needs has improved is that of deriving these needs from the purpose, objectives and performance requirements of the organization. Instead of providing training needs analysis against some hypothetical belief of what managers should do, or even a behaviourally based training needs analysis based on what managers currently are doing, the better training and development professionals now always turn to some means of analysing the needs of the organization first. One consequence of this approach is that any development needs are firmly attached to real organizational requirements rather than to general statements of 'what all managers need to be able to do'. In that sense it is essentially the same as the more individually based ideas mentioned in previous chapters. Instead, for example, of adopting this year's favourite management development activity, whether it be customer care, service quality standards or leadership, the line manager can assist with identifying the essential issues and the priorities involved in them.

Customer Care is an example of this approach, as shown in Chart 10.1.

Chart 10.1   Identifying training requirements for Customer Care

1. Who are our customers?
2. Do we have intermediaries between ourselves and customers?
3. What external data do we have on customer reactions to our service?
4. What internal data do we have on customer reactions?
5. What information do we have on competitor service levels and reactions to customers?
6. What are the main priorities for improving Customer Care?
7. What are the main methods to be employed?
8. Is there a difference between what managers need to do in future, and their current level of skills, knowledge, attitudes or insight?

The business plan ought to indicate what kind of customers are being sought, what the issues are about customer relationships, and what the opportunities and what the problems are.

Many managers will now have experienced some version of the SWOT analysis – Strengths, Weaknesses, Opportunities, Threats. Earlier, in Chapter 9, at an individual level the idea of OPP – Opportunities, Problems and

Priorities – was offered as an alternative. Managers should use their own managerial statements, disciplines and controls to produce the initial statement of what is needed.

The business plan or SWOT approach is particularly relevant in organizations undergoing change. Thus we see the contribution of managers in identifying, for example, in British Airways, the shift of behaviour needed following their identification that customer service would give them a competitive edge, as compared with using price. Training in improved customer service then followed the business plan rather than some general belief, often copied from other organizations, that customer service is a good idea.

In organizations transforming themselves from public sector to private sector, managers can and should participate in the process of defining what kind of changes in managerial behaviour, attitude and skills are required by the move. Of course it is best if this process is initiated at the top, and involves full participation there. I worked with what had been the Executive Committee but was to become the Board of a public sector company about to be privatized. The contribution of these top managers was two-fold. First they identified the changes in their behaviour and practices that would be necessary, and secondly they discussed the implications of these changes for the managers under them.

These two examples give some idea of two alternatives in looking at how an organization's purpose and business plan can be used to identify development needs and therefore the kind of help that ought to be provided. The first is the more traditional format of a business plan being produced and development needs identified as a consequence. The second centres on the use of ongoing reviews of strategy and needs as an integrated process. In effect managers or directors working on their own problems produce both answers to those problems and development for themselves and for others. This is the Action Learning approach which I strongly favour. My own work is built on a diagnostic interview with managers, based on topics for discussion. The topics vary according to my remit and the organization, as illustrated in Chart 10.2.

Chart 10.2   Director development needs – Topics for discussion

1. What is the main purpose of your business?
2. What do you see as the main issues influencing performance at your level in the organization?
3. What do you think the main issues are likely to be over the next two years?
4. Is there a strategy and business plan designed to manage these issues?
5. Is there an up-to-date statement of the content and priorities for your job?
6. Is your personal performance formally reviewed?
7. What kinds of skill, knowledge and experience do you believe are necessary to manage these issues now, and in the future?
8. How well equipped do you believe you and your colleagues are on these requirements?
9. Do you have any other comments to make relevant to this discussion?

What Kind of General Needs?

The first part of this chapter emphasized the dangers of generalizing about needs and solutions. The usual answer is to create a course to meet some identified need. Just as it is true to say that at some level of generalization all managers do the same kind of job, it is the case that groups of managers have similar skill or knowledge requirements. Organizations will therefore run for themselves, or send their managers to, it is hoped, reputable external courses dealing with issues such as Effective Speaking, Finance for Non-Financial Managers, Effective Teamwork, and Quality Assurance in the 1990s. All too often, these courses fall into one of two categories. They represent a managerial version of a sheep dip, in which managers are thrust through some cleansing process designed to eliminate managerial sickness or disease. Alternatively, they are equivalent to the, perhaps apocryphal, Chinese general who baptized his army into Christianity with a hose, the analogy this time being more that of washing good practices in rather than washing bad practices out. Line managers themselves contribute to these mistakes, and indeed often stimulate and encourage them by putting the wrong kind of pressure on professional providers. 'I want all my people to go through Course X over the next twelve months.' 'The problem round here is that our staff do not know the difference between assertiveness and aggressiveness – see if you can get that woman who ran the sessions on that course we went on last year to run courses for us.'

EXERCISE 10.1

1. Have you been involved recently in the production of a business plan or similar task?
2. Has it been used as a way of determining development needs and priorities for meeting them?
3. Have you been involved within the last 12 months in helping to define needs to be met through a course to be run for a group or groups of managers?
4. Review the comments made so far in this chapter; are you now satisfied with the contribution you have been asked to make?
5. Can you formulate some questions that you now want to put to your professional management development advisers?

Designing Problem Centred Workshops

The prime need is always for the line manager to be analytical and careful about identifying what the need really is. The second need is to take the risk in pursuit of the greater benefits involved in running events which will be described as workshops rather than courses. Managers should demand or be responsive to suggestions from their professional advisers that learning and development events use real managerial work as the core of the process. They should challenge statements about the quantity of formal input that is required, how much knowledge people will need before they can tackle real problems, and the view that off-the-job experiences should concentrate on 'learning', rather than implementation. The defects of traditional training and education are gradually, but too slowly, being challenged by the more sophisticated and up-to-date professionals. Managers should insist that groups work on real management problems, and should not accept that an off-the-job training or educational experience cannot deal with such issues or that this is not the best use of time. Trainers and educators have helped to create a massive problem of transfer from an off-the-job learning experience to on-the-job reality, and then blame the receiving managers for failing to resolve the problem they have created. Line managers can help ensure that the failure to transfer learning problems does not arise in the first place, by insisting that off-the-job content should work through real management opportunities and problems. Chart 10.3 gives an abbreviated version of an in-company workshop I have run on 'Change'.

Chart 10.3   An example of a problem centred workshop

1. **Preparation**
1.1 Look back over your experiences of change. Select three examples:
    • What were the causes of change?
    • Who were the managers of the change process?
    • What were the objectives of change?
    • How successful was the change?
1.2 Look at a recent or current change experience which you are managing. Prepare to present your views on this at the workshop.
1.3 Prepare to present a current change problem to a colleague at the workshop.
2. **Workshop Content**
    What are the factors driving change in your organization?
    What is helpful in bringing about effective change?
    What hinders effective change?
    What other lessons have you learned from your own experience?
    How do we compare with Kanter's 'Rules for Stifling Innovation'.
    How can I manage a current change problem/opportunity more effectively?

Learning, Development and Helping as Group Needs

The subject of this book is an example of potential needs for groups of managers as well as individuals.

It is relatively recent that learning as a process has received serious attention in management development systems and programmes. One of the ways of highlighting the issues and improving the capacity of managers to help each other learn is 'to run a course'. A number of organizations run programmes on the roles and skills identified in earlier chapters for coaches and mentors. Even more run courses on appraisal. It seems they are more often initiated by advisers who think managers ought to improve their skills, than by managers when they are asked to carry out coaching and mentoring as a formal management development activity.

In Chapter 8 it was suggested that manager developers could form a learning group to discuss their experiences. This would be a development effort created by a group to meet a defined need. An extension of this idea could be, as in the case of coaching and mentoring, the design of courses or workshops on the issues and opportunities of a broader developmental thrust indicated through this book.

It is interesting to compare the proliferation of courses on Finance for Non-Financial Managers with the absence of courses on, for example, Developing Myself and Others. In terms of likely practical application, the proportion ought to be exactly the reverse! Although I favour the development of such courses, the principle still applies of testing the need by some diagnosis of what managers are required to do. Manager developers should ask for such courses because they feel a need for them, not just because an adviser tells them 'all managers ought to be good developers'.

An example of a workshop on this theme is given in Chart 10.4.

Chart 10.4   Helpers in management development

- Different roles as Boss, Mentor, Coach, Problem Counsellor, Grand Boss, Client and Sponsor.
- What does help mean to the different participants?
- How to use normal work experiences for development – Projects, Ongoing Problems, Tasks, Meetings.
- How to identify individual learner preferences and relate learning opportunities to them (Learning Styles Questionnaire).
- How to identify and work on different kinds of learning opportunity off the job and through the job.
- How to identify obstacles to learning such as skills of learning, attitudes and emotions, the working situation (Learning Diagnostic Questionnaire).

This is a one- or two-day workshop. It can be run either for managers at one level, or for manager/subordinate pairs.

EXERCISE 10.2   FORMAL DEVELOPMENT AS A DEVELOPER

1. Have you had experience of attending a course/workshop designed to help you carry out your responsibilities as a developer of others (e.g. Appraisal, Coaching, Mentoring)?
2. How did you feel about that experience at the time?
3. What do you feel about the experience now, in the light of what you have read in this book?
4. If you have had no formal training for these responsibilities, do you think it might be helpful (see Chart 10.4 as one illustration)?
5. Is there any action you should take as a result of your conclusions to (3) and (4) above?

Contributing to Courses

As has already been implied, the main contribution of the helping manager is to ensure that the content of any course is relevant, appropriate and usable. It is in this that the role of the helping manager really can centre on the group rather than on the individual. However, what is being asked here is for the surrender of two of the manager's most treasured possessions. The first is security. The more general, conceptual, knowledge based a course is, the greater the security of managers who are unlikely to be challenged either as participants or as sponsors by ideas or techniques whose practicality is so evident that the sponsoring manager will have great difficulty in rejecting the idea. The virtues of reality come with the price of genuine commitment to looking at problems uncovered, opportunities created and solutions advanced. The second surrender is that of the precious commodity of time. It will often seem a lot easier for the line manager to pass responsibility not only for the design but for the content of courses over to the professionals, because anything else involves a significant allocation of time to discuss what the organization needs and what the solutions might be. Of course, the pay-off from such involvements is dramatically better than will be achieved through any other route – but like many other pay-offs in management development it tends to be longer term and therefore less attractive to some managers.

It is much easier, for managers to be involved in a course or workshop itself. Usually this is formally by means of presenting a talk, listening to a presentation from syndicates or reviewing a case study. In my experience, these are powerful and important ways of involving line managers not only because they bring the heat of genuine management problems to the sometimes over-rational and objective conduct of a course. The other aspect is that the participation of the line manager is a physical demonstration of some kind of commitment to what is going on. As a course participant once said to me, 'I am sure you could have done a better job at summarizing the presentations and picking the bones out. But the important thing was that he bothered to travel a long way in a busy week to come. It told us something about how important he thought this occasion was'.

Finally there is the social element in the contribution that managers can make. Relatively informal participation over drinks or over meals can sometimes have a surprising effect. People will remember a sentence or two in the bar whilst they will forget a similar contribution expressed didactically in a formal session. Naturally the intelligent and sensitive line manager will recognize that minority of course participants who want to use the occasion to sell themselves as high quality performers.

Managing the System

As with any other aspect of management, the issue on which line managers can help themselves and others most directly is in ensuring that objectives, priorities and standards for performance are set, monitored and changed when necessary. My research shows a devastating lack of effort to undertake this. My inclination is to blame the management development professionals for not proposing methods in this area (and I mean the complete system, not just evaluating the success of courses). However, line managers must also be criticized for failure here in what they require in all the other areas for which they are responsible as managers. If you set up a system which is designed to produce managers who have been, for example, taken through a particular development process, it does not seem too challenging a proposition that there should be methods of assessing whether this has actually happened or not.

If you have an element in your Appraisal System which is designed to assess which people have potential, it seems rather basic that you should at some time review how accurate the predictions have been (or rather at what level of inaccuracy since research shows how faulty predictions often are). If a monitoring process existed, there would be fewer organizations annually going through the often grotesquely inefficient and ineffective process called Succession Planning. Perhaps line managers participate in this relatively willingly because it is all too often a kind of detached unreal decision making with no consequences in many cases. Hypothetical decisions about who might succeed where all too often are not followed by real later decisions. This is not to say that Succession Planning or, as I advocate, the larger-scale Resource Planning, is an inappropriate element in a management development system; it should be emphasized again that the value of a system has to be assessed if it is to be meaningful rather than a paper charade.

Designing Systems and Recognizing Opportunities

In addition to the design and implementation of courses the line manager should help with the development of processes for appraisal or performance review of the identification of potential. Again the contribution is essentially one of making these processes 'honest' in managerial terms, i.e. capable of being understood and used by line managers rather than representing the most up-to-date views about what sophisticated management development should look like.

At least equally important is the involvement of managers in making better use not only at individual but at group level of learning opportunities as shown in Chapter 8. The idea of changing Big O into managed learning opportunities applies, of course, to groups as well as to individuals. The technique of a learning process review at the end of meetings, of establishing some process for reviewing the reasons for success or failure which we have commented on in earlier chapters, is very important. Indeed it contributes through the effective development of useful practices within particular groups to the eventual evolution of the learning organization. It is only through the creation of effective practices, first for individuals and then for groups, that the large-scale proposals about creating effective Learning Organizations will actually be achieved.

Again we can remember that the technique suggested here is essentially only a development of what good managers do anyway – which is to review what has happened, why it has happened, what the causes of success and failure were and the lessons to be drawn for the future. They probably call it a task review or a project review, but a greater emphasis on the additional aspects of 'what we have learned from the experience' helps create a management development system based firmly on the reality of what managers actually do.

Written Material as a Means of Meeting Group Needs

Courses are not the only resources available as aids to the development of managers. Books are perhaps the most familiar, sometimes promoted as bestsellers that everyone should read. Some organizations provide policies, guidelines and workbooks aimed at managers in general. These can all be helpful, but they are most useful if they are integrated with some more active development process.

Priorities for the Manager Developer

The size and detail of this chapter compared with the previous one indicate where I think the priorities for manager developers both are and ought to be.

It is not that the issues of group type manager development are unimportant, nor is it that the contributions of managers to this are of little significance – the main points made in this chapter show how vital these contributions are to effectiveness. It is rather that their input at individual level is what makes the large scale systems work.

Further, most managers recollect their experiences in helping or being helped in individual relationships. They are unlikely to identify the system which helped. Nor are they likely to highlight their managerial contribution as being on the design of an Appraisal System, or a course. While it may be, as argued here, that they often have been insufficiently involved in such issues, it is the interaction with individuals that will always matter most.

Finally, if we look again at the reasons why managers are interested in developing other managers, expressed under the Principle of Reciprocity, we see that this is infrequently present in working on general group issues. The direct return in immediate manager performance, or the personal satisfaction in having 'brought someone on', is clearly less available in group diagnosed and centred activities.

11

How to be helped

Chapter 5 dealt with the question of what different individuals mean by help. Now that we have considered the kind of help offered through the formal management development system, it is possible to extend the discussion of how individuals react to help.

'You can take a horse to water, but you can't make it drink' – folk wisdom.

'I am always willing to learn, but I do not always like being taught' – attributed to Sir Winston Churchill.

'I have given every kind of help you can think of – he won't use any of it' – manager to the author.

'He thinks telling me in great detail how to do the job is being helpful' – subordinate of same manager to author.

'She went to a lot of trouble to find out not what I needed but what I would accept in the way of help' – another subordinate, about another manager.

Help is defined by the learner, not by the helper, as emphasized earlier in this book. This is not easy to put into effect for several reasons, including:

- The drive for immediate managerial performance tends to make the manager impatient, therefore to offer help that is 'clearly required'.
- The more junior manager – the learner – may be reluctant to state needs clearly, and also reluctant to spell out in what form helping with those needs would be acceptable.
- The characteristic emphasis of managers on task and performance rather than on process and relationships inhibits where it does not absolutely prevent discussion of what 'help' actually means.
- Managers usually work from themselves outwards. They operate by their definition and understanding of problems, opportunities and needs. Even

more important, they operate according to their views of how they would be helped in how to learn. They do not usually try to operate from the perspective of the learner.

In order better to understand and test these propositions, the manager developer should tackle the following two exercises.

EXERCISE 11.1   AN EXPERIENCE OF BEING HELPED

Look back over your managerial career and find an example where you were helped to learn something by a boss, mentor, colleague or subordinate. The occasion may have arisen through a formal discussion, e.g. appraisal, Personal Development Plan, being mentored or coached. It may have been an informal, relatively accidental experience – discussing a problem or a potential situation.

1.   What was the issue, problem or need which led to your being helped?
2.   Did you recognize in advance that you might benefit from some help?
3.   Why do you think the other person involved gave you some help?
4.   What were your strongest reasons for accepting the help that was offered?
5.   What feelings did you have about the way in which help was offered?
6.   What skills do you think your helper displayed?

You might wish to review your answers to this exercise in more detail by looking back at the statements on pages 101 and 105 about the skills displayed by helpers.

EXERCISE 11.2   AN EXPERIENCE OF NOT BEING HELPED

Look back on your managerial career and see if you can identify an occasion on which someone attempted to offer you help, which you were unable to use.

1.   What was the issue, problem or need involved?
2.   Why did you think that some kind of help might be useful?
3.   Why do you think the helper was trying to give help?
4.   What feelings did you have while help was being offered?
5.   What skills were displayed or not displayed by the helper?
6.   What other reasons do you have for feeling that this was an unsuccessful experience in helping?

It is reasonable to assume that when someone offers help, the offer is made as a constructive proposal, rather than as an attempt to destroy the confidence of the other person. We can also assume that the person who offers the help does not intend to create a situation in which the learner takes a negative view of the helper. It is much more likely that the helper's intention is both genuinely to help and also involves some degree of ego-satisfaction on the part of the helper – it is gratifying to feel that you have 'brought someone on', or 'helped that young man to develop his skills early in his career'. So, if we can assume that intentions are on the whole honourable, as they clearly will be for anyone reading this book, then we need to examine more intensively the reasons why things can go wrong – as well as why they can go right. Reactions to Exercises 11.1 and 11.2 are part of the process for establishing this. It is only part of the picture, of course, because it deals with your reaction to being helped, which it was suggested early on might not be the reaction of another individual in the same situation. In order to increase awareness of possible differences in offering as compared with receiving help, the following two exercises will help.

EXERCISE 11.3   A SUCCESSFUL EXPERIENCE OF OFFERING HELP

1. What was the issue, problem or need on which you were attempting to offer help?
2. Why were you offering help?
3. Why do you think the other person was interested in being helped?
4. What feelings did you have while you were offering help?
5. What evidence was there about the feelings of the person you were trying to help?
6. What skills do you think were involved on your part?
7. What made this into a successful helping experience?

EXERCISE 11.4   AN UNSUCCESSFUL EXPERIENCE OF OFFERING HELP

1. What was the issue, problem or need on which you were attempting to offer help?
2. Why were you offering help?
3. Why do you think the other person was interested in being helped?
4. What feelings did you have while you were offering help?
5. What evidence was there about the feelings of the person you were trying to help?
6. What skills do you think were displayed or not displayed?
7. What other reasons do you have for feeling that this was an unsuccessful experience in helping?

The next stage is to draw general conclusions from Exercises 11.1–11.4.

EXERCISE 11.5   DRAWING CONCLUSIONS ABOUT HELPING

1. Do you think there are any general lessons to be drawn about how you might offer help?
2. How do your experiences match, or differ from, those suggested at the

beginning of this chapter as reasons why help is either not offered, or offered unsuccessfully?

The final stage in this process is to decide what you will do as a result of the review of your experiences and the conclusions you have drawn. This can be done as a general course of action, or specifically in relation to a particular individual:

3. What kind of things will you watch out for when attempting to offer help to someone else in future?
4. What points strike you as particularly important in relation to a specific individual to whom you might be offering help in the future?

The sequence of activities presented in this chapter so far may now be familiar. The Learning Cycle has been in operation (Figure 11.1). Readers who have attempted the exercises and the follow-up questions have been encouraged to go along a path which then can be seen formally as a Learning Cycle. The reflecting and reviewing stage will almost certainly have been deeper and more careful than what they may have attempted or understood previously about their experiences of being helped or helping.

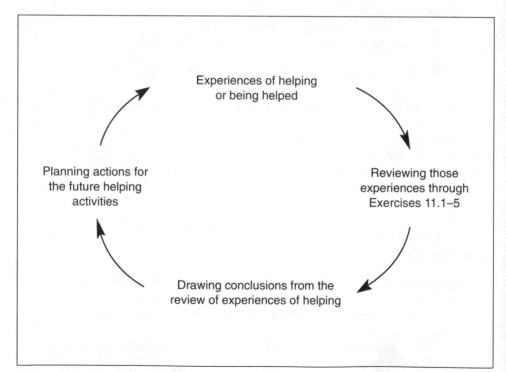

Experiences of helping
or being helped

Reviewing those
experiences through
Exercises 11.1–5

Drawing conclusions from the
review of experiences of helping

Planning actions for
the future helping
activities

Figure 11.1 The Learning Cycle and helping

Similarly, the individual learner will have been round the Learning Cycle. The learner's reflections on even the same experience will be different because they will perceive it differently, and their conclusions and plans for subsequent action will be different also.

On several occasions in this book the desirability of encouraging explicit attention to the stages of the Learning Cycle, and actions which contribute to effective learning through each stage, has been emphasized. It has been suggested that careful attention to each stage of the Learning Cycle will bring benefits in achieved learning. It has also been pointed out that individuals vary in their interest or willingness to devote serious attention to the different stages of the Learning Cycle.

One example of this may be found by the reaction of different individuals to the construction of this chapter so far. Some readers will have valued the idea of reviewing their personal experiences both as helper and learner, and the relatively slow build-up towards conclusions and plans for action. Other readers will have impatiently waited for the stage at which 'practical suggestions' are made. 'I know people are different. Why don't you just get on with telling me how to recognize and deal with the differences?' So if the approach so far may have been attractive to Reflectors, the next sections aim to seize the attention of Pragmatists.

What Kind of Learner am I Helping?

Help is defined by the learner, both in the kind of help and how the help is offered. Individual reactions to being helped to learn derive from (especially but not solely) Learning Style preferences.

Case Study 1

An individual with a strong Reflector Learning Style was promoted to a new job in a different part of the company and in a different part of the country. 'I can never get my boss to sit down with me and talk through problems. Say I want to discuss something, he is as likely as not to give me a snap answer on the phone. That's no good to me. I want to chew things over.' The boss involved was a strong Activist.

Case Study 2

The Managing Director of a company had taken a Master of Business Administration programme at a prestigious business school. He regarded it as a superb experience which all managers of high potential should go through.

He was a strong Theorist.

The response of one of his managers sent on a similar MBA programme was 'It was a stretching experience for me intellectually. I enjoyed attacking some big problems, using models, concepts and theories that were showered on us during the course'. This manager, too, was a strong Theorist. The reaction of another manager was 'I know the intention of sending me on the programme was good. But it really didn't help me significantly. So many of the examples we studied in great depth were taken from industries quite different from ours. I thought there was a lot of intellectual games-playing that went on between some of the participants and the Professors. The boss talked about me stretching my mind as a result of the programme. I would have preferred to stretch it by looking at things which were much more realistic and relevant to this particular company'.

This individual was a strong Pragmatist.

Case Study 3

'During my appraisal, my boss set a subsequent date for me to draw up a Personal Development Plan with him. We did that, and in the course of it he suggested that I should keep a diary of the significant things I was involved in and what I was learning from them. We used to meet twice a month over a sandwich lunch in his office, and I would go over all the things I had been involved in and what I had learned. I know he offered the same kind of thing to one or two of my colleagues but they didn't take him up or, in one case, dropped out very quickly. I think it was the fact that it turned out we were both strong Reflectors that made the kind of help he offered very acceptable to me.'

Case Study 4

'My boss was called "Jumping Jack" because he never stood still for a moment. He was always roaring around dealing with problems and sorting out difficulties. It was tremendously exciting to be with him. He gave you plenty of opportunities as well. He would throw three things at you and just tell you to get on with them and only come back to him if you were on the point of death. I enjoyed the responsibility. But then everybody thought I was very similar to him, except that I was a woman, so there were a lot of jokes about "Jack and Jill".'

'Jack and Jill' in this case were strong Activists.

The cases should have demonstrated that help is more likely to be accepted and welcome if it is offered in the mode of learning preferred by the learner. As has been said earlier in this book, this is not necessarily a finally limiting position. Of course, it is desirable for the strong Activist to be encouraged to be more analytical, to collect more data, to think harder – in other words to improve their capacity as Reflectors – but the most effective starting point for most helpers will be to offer help in the style most likely to be accepted by the learner.

A more ambitious relationship can certainly be developed, especially when both parties know each other's strengths. It is quite possible for a strong

Activist to help a strong Reflector by encouraging that person to take advantage of immediate and accidental opportunities. In the reverse situation, it is possible for the strong Reflector boss to encourage the strong Activist learner to collect his or her thoughts occasionally.

In both cases, the likely productive development is best described as incremental, rather than transformational; steps rather than leaps. The helper should not ask the learner to undergo a total transformation in preferred methods of learning. It is not surprising that a strong Activist would not accept readily the idea of regular review meetings even over an informal lunch (Case 3). What the strong Reflector manager might more appropriately offer is opportunities to talk things over immediately after significant experiences – to seize the moment, rather than plan for a week's experiences. Similarly, the strongly Activist boss, mentor or coach, could encourage the strongly Reflective learner towards occasional experimentation with something unusual, exciting and unplanned, rather than constantly throwing up a barrage of such opportunities.

EXERCISE 11.6   LEARNING STYLES AND BEING HELPED

Look back at the experiences in Exercises 11.1–5.

1. Do you think your own preferred Learning Style (see page 56) has had an influence on what you have offered and how you have offered it?
2. Do you think the Learning Style of the individual to whom you have offered help matched your preferred style?
3. Do you think similarities between you may explain success?
4. Do you think dissimilarities in your Learning Styles may help you explain a lack of success?
5. Look again at the individual you thought about when developing your action plan earlier in this chapter on pages 169–70. Are any changes necessary in view of your own Learning Style preferences and those of the individual you have selected?

The Learning Diagnostic Questionnaire

In Chapter 5 we considered organizational and personal barriers to learning, and how these might be revealed by the Learning Diagnostic Questionnaire (see Further Reading). The Attitudes and Emotions section of the Learning Diagnostic Questionnaire is clearly significant in terms of the reactions of individuals to being helped. If an individual does not recognize the need for help, then the offer of help is unlikely to be taken up. The following paired questions from the LDQ indicate whether an individual might be responsive to help in a situation where the need is not absolutely obvious:

When things are going well, I tend to leave them alone.

Or,
When things are going well, I look for ways to get them to go even better.

A rather different example:

I am fascinated to find out about myself.
Or,
I am disinclined to look into myself too deeply.

In addition to this information, which helps to establish some of the personal beliefs which may influence willingness to accept help, the LDQ, as again we have seen in Chapter 5, offers help on the organizational context. One of the issues about asking for or accepting help is that the individual learner will have a view about the seriousness of any offer of help. Is the offer of help congruent with apparent organizational beliefs about learning, or different from those beliefs? The questions on Working Situation in the LDQ, several of which were given in Chapter 5, will indicate the feelings of the individual about the organization.

Like the Learning Styles Questionnaire, the Learning Diagnostic Questionnaire gives the helping manager an objective basis for discussing these issues with the individual who is to be helped. Instead of the assumptions and half-communications on which views about the learner are all too often based, these instruments allow for the review of specific, concrete factors affecting the likely reception of help on learning.

Other Information on the Learner

The LSQ and LDQ have been placed in the forefront of this section because they are objective instruments, and because they are specifically looking at learning processes. Of course, there is a volume of other information about the potential learner to be considered:

- Observation of how the individual has responded to previous offers of help from yourself, or from others.
- Observation of general characteristics of behaviour in the managerial environment – 'management style'.
- Interactions on individual performance review/appraisal.
- Interactions on Personal Development Plan/Learning Agreement.
- Data from other diagnostic questionnaires. Increasingly, organizations make use of various tests of personal qualities and skills. They may provide clues in addition to their prime use on how an individual may react to being helped to learn. Although instruments such as the Myers Briggs Type Indicator, the Margerison McCann Team Management Index, Cattell's 16PF and the variety of Saville and Holdsworth questionnaires produce valid information for the purposes for which they are designed,

great care should be taken in extending their use into the learning area. Specifically, the personality assessments, which might seem to present the clearest clues, ought only to be interpreted by those professionally competent to do so.

All this information can be drawn together in order to create a view about how a learner might react to different kinds of help.

The appraisal and Personal Development Plan discussions and documents ought to be the best indicator, at least at the level of showing the areas in which an individual wishes to be helped. It is worth emphasizing, however, that these processes are usually better at identifying needs than at securing understanding of and commitment to the processes involved in meeting the needs. For example, appraisal might include the following:

'So we have agreed, Jane, that your skills of chairing meetings could be developed. We will have another attempt later to find a good course for you.'

Or, through the same appraisal interview, a rather different method might be proposed:

'So we have agreed, Jane, that your skills of chairing meetings could be developed. The best thing would be to ask for comments from John after each meeting – he's an experienced guy who I am sure can help you.'

What these two examples demonstrate is that even when an individual has reached an understanding of, and a commitment to the need for help on, a managerial need, different kinds of help would produce possibly different kinds of reaction. Sending someone on a course may often seem the obvious and indeed the best solution – the opportunity to practise skills in a relatively secure environment. But do Jane's Learning Style preferences match the methods used on the course?

The idea of feedback and coaching on the job, on the other hand, although potentially much more realistic, is also much less secure. Can John give constructive feedback effectively? Can he do so in a way which might then lead to further discussion or coaching? How do Jane's Learning Styles relate to John's, and to the process of feedback and coaching?

Indicators of Positive Attitudes to Help

Most managers have personal characteristics which are helpful in some situations and unhelpful in others. For example, the characteristic sometimes described as 'get up and go' can be very useful in many situations, but can be unhelpful in a situation where the real requirement is to sort out a tangled series of complex issues, or to think long term. In the same way, there are some characteristics managers may have which are desirable for their managerial role, but which need to be balanced by other characteristics if they are to be capable of receiving help. Chart 11.1 illustrates some of these characteristics.

Chart 11.1   Balancing characteristics in accepting help

Characteristic	Balanced By
Strong, clear self-image	Openness to data about self-image from others
Capacity to work alone	Acceptance of a degree of dependence on others
Capacity to make clear, firm decision on demand	Openness to new and different ideas
Core feeling 'I am a competent manager'	'I could be better'
'As a manager, I have to show I know what to do'	'Sometimes I can say I don't know what to do'
Development is up to the individual	Individuals can be helped to develop.

Reactions to Different Helpers

The different contributions of boss, mentor, colleagues and subordinates have been reviewed in earlier chapters. Some managers find it easier to be helped by mentors or someone else outside the direct managerial line. While the line relationship to the manager's boss presents the clearest opportunities and the sharpest understanding of what is involved, that relationship is also fundamentally geared to views about performance. Understandably, not all managers are prepared to reveal all their weaknesses or feelings about being helped to a boss who is going to write the performance review and recommend a salary increase – or otherwise.

One of the problems about a helping relationship between a line manager and a subordinate is that it may require a shift in that relationship, which in practice neither party manages terribly well. A manager may be used to receiving from her boss a series of crisp, no-nonsense, unarguable decisions, or specific statements about what to do and how to do it. A sudden transition to a special session in which the emphasis shifts to development, and the boss suddenly becomes a reflective, careful, sensitive listener to the subordinate's problems, is often unsuccessful for both parties. Managers should, therefore, consider their characteristic style and the probable impact this has had on someone whom they wish to help in order to consider the likely reaction of the potential learner.

Gender Differences and Help

Another consideration about the helper which affects likely reactions arises when the genders are different. A male boss with a female learner or a female boss with a male learner can cause problems which are different from those which may be experienced by participants of the same gender. The difficulty here lies in recognizing the reality of actual or potential reactions, rather than importing stereotypes related to gender differences and assuming that the stereotype is true.

It is a requirement to consider the individual first, and to consider gender differences second in order to avoid this. This means thinking of Jane as an individual with specific data about her from the instruments mentioned above and from her past history. The reason for emphasizing this approach is that many male managers have attitudes and behaviours based on stereotypical views of 'all women'. The help they offer may therefore be presented in a style which is inappropriate for the individual woman learner and quite possibly unintentionally insulting. Here are some examples:

- 'You have to wrap up feedback to women. If you give them direct chapter and verse, they cry.'
- 'She is a great asset to the team; like all women, she has great strengths of intuition.'
- 'I concentrated on short-term development with her. I knew it was a waste of time talking about her longer-term career as soon as she married.'

In all three cases the manager was assuming a generalized woman's reaction, rather than establishing what the interests and capacities of the particular 'manager who happens to be a woman' might have been.

There are many other issues affecting the kind of help women are offered, or should be offered. One of particular relevance to this chapter is whether they should be offered different kinds of opportunity, or be given special preference. Another is whether women as a group differ from men in their preferred styles of learning.

I have already suggested that both men and women should be treated as individuals first, not as representatives of a gender stereotype. This is different from saying that there is no need for special action to enable women to overcome the disadvantages they face in a predominantly male orientated managerial world. My own belief is that the forces of conservatism and inertia are such that action to identify and develop women managers as a group is necessary. There are, for example, strong arguments for 'women only' management courses, especially if these are additional to, not a replacement for, courses also attended by male managers.

This issue connects with the question of preferred ways of learning. The data secured from the Learning Styles Questionnaire shows that there is no significant difference between men as a group and women as a group. Men are not more Activist, women are not more Reflector.

An interesting study from the United States by Van Velsor and Hughes (see Further Reading) shows that men and women differ in some respects in what they learn. There are some differences in what they report as learning, for example, women refer more frequently to learning about personal limits and blind spots. Especially fascinating in the context of this book, they also identify recognizing and seizing learning opportunities.

The study also reports that whereas 18 per cent of men reported at least one event centred on learning from another person, 51 per cent of women did so. If replicated in larger numbers and in other countries, this finding would indicate an area of great advantage for women.

There are fewer women who have male subordinates, but the same considerations about stereotypes apply:

- 'He is a typical man – power-hungry with no sensitivity to the needs of others.'
- 'Of course, this is a macho man culture here, and Stephen fits into it beautifully.'
- 'Because he is a man and I am a woman, he finds it impossible to accept help from me.'

Some readers may find these statements accurate and acceptable. That is, of course, a statement about stereotypes – they contain enough truths to be generally believed to be true at some stage. What must be remembered is that using stereotypes always contains the possibility of error, and in regard to relationships of the kind discussed in this chapter, the application of stereotypes prevents dealing with the individual.

The last quotation given above is of relevance, because it is easy to accept as likely. The question to be asked, however, concerning the reaction of the individual to any offer of help, is whether that individual is actually responding as a male subordinate to a female boss, or as an individual whose personality and behaviour inhibits acceptance of help from anyone – man or woman. Or could it be that the style of the manager developer inhibits acceptance of help by anyone – man or woman.

Ethnic and National Differences

Fortunately, the extension of managerial opportunities to women is increasingly creating experiences showing that stereotypes about them are often untrue and unhelpful. Quantitatively, the same cannot yet be said about the other area in which Equal Opportunities has been growing – the managers from ethnic minorities. The problems of offering and receiving help match those of the male/female relationship in complexity of issues and emotion. The same issues of stereotypes occur:

'Of course, it's useless to talk to him about managing his time more effectively – it is simply not important in his culture.'

Similar problems can arise on differences of national culture where the colour of the skin may be the same, but stereotypes about types of national behaviour exist:

- 'Like all Germans, he believed in systems, order, procedures and rules. It was hopeless to think of talking to him about handling one individual differently from another.'
- 'He was a typical Italian. You know how they have two sets of accounts, one the real thing, the other that they present to the tax inspector. He had two managerial styles, depending on whether he was talking to his boss or his subordinates.'

The issues of significant differences affected by gender, race, national culture and others not covered above, such as religion, have a fundamental influence. We are more likely to take effective helping action if we consider people as individuals first, and view their actual behaviour as individuals, before we attribute causes and explanations based on these larger constructs.

EXERCISE 11.6   HANDLING DIFFERENCES

1. Do you have experience of offering help to someone who differs from you in gender, ethnic or national origin?
2. Do you think the content and style of help you have offered has been influenced by your general views about people with those origins?
3. Have you encountered difficulties which you believe you have not encountered with individuals whose origins are similar to your own?
4. What have you learned as a result of the experience?

One More Time – The Learner Defines Help

Good intentions are insufficient to produce an effective helping relationship. They are a necessary but insufficient condition. There is the story of the Boy Scout who gave artificial respiration to a boy who had fallen into a pond. 'I tried to give him artificial respiration, but he kept getting up and saying he wanted to change his clothes.' If the form, content and process of the help being offered are not relevant to the learner's needs, and congruent with the learner's preferred way of learning, the learner will reject the proffered help.

12

Develop yourself

As we have considered each issue through this book, the exercises provided have often started with the manager developer rather than immediately turning to things that can be done with the learner. The reasons for this have been:

- Developers will give more effective assistance if they have reviewed and interpreted their own equivalent experiences before they try to help someone else.
- Developers ought to learn something which is relevant and useful for their own development.
- The provision of these exercises reinforces a basic point about the nature of the help being offered.

Management development has moved away from a directive insistence from some expert – whether facilitator or manager – who knows best what the development need is and how it should be met. We now operate much more on the basis of acceptance of responsibility by the individual as the prime participant in a process of development, rather than the recipient of someone else's planned teaching. It is a fundamental and difficult shift from a process 'done to' managers to a process in which management development is 'done with' managers.

Throughout this book, the assumption have been that the learner will do more than accept needs or processes defined for the learner by someone more experienced or more expert. The philosophy and the detailed practice have both been about encouraging self-development – in which the learner takes responsibility for identifying needs, for recognizing opportunities, for selecting methods of learning appropriate to the learner. The combination of involvement and responsibility generates commitment to personal action, instead of acceptance of the need to follow someone else's prescription.

If the philosophy and practices of self-development are to be fully meaningful in the context of one person helping another, the manager developer needs to adopt those same principles and actions for her or his own self-development.

As already indicated, one reason for suggesting that developers undertake exercises throughout this book directed at their own situation and opportunities is that this gives them experience in the techniques and activities they may suggest for others. They will then experience both the opportunities and problems opened out through the approaches suggested here.

A second and strongly associated reason is that by doing the work suggested for themselves, managers will confirm the validity of the ideas suggested. There is nothing like the personal recognition of how completing an exercise has benefited you as a means of convincing you about the significance and depth of some of the answers that may emerge when you try to help others.

Thirdly, the fact that developers can talk from their own experience of having completed work on themselves enables them to describe, talk about and respond to questions on their own beliefs about the process on offer, in a way which gives colour, conviction and credibility. If we take an apparently similar experience, that of appraisal, it is extremely demotivating to be appraised by someone who is going through the motions with no real belief in the virtues of careful performance review.

All these are good reasons why managers undertaking the exercises in this book will be better able to help others. In addition, the process contains virtues in that it delivers something of direct value to developers themselves. Managers can develop themselves through the process of trying to develop others.

EXERCISE 12.1   SELF-DEVELOPMENT AS A PRECURSOR TO DEVELOPING OTHERS

1. Here are the five reasons why self-development through exercises earlier in this book is an essential part of the process of helping others:

    a) Experiencing the kind of opportunities and problems involved in the approach.
    b) Recognizing the problems other people may have in 'doing it'.
    c) Testing the validity of the whole approach for yourself.
    d) Providing credibility from your own experience in what you offer to others.
    e) Personal development achieved through the exercises.

2. Put your own priorities on each of these, starting with 1 for the statement which you believe to be most important and 5 for the one of least significance.

3. Are there any other reasons you can identify why carrying out the approaches on yourself will be helpful in enabling you to help others?

Basically developers who have completed at least so
related to their own experiences, as well as those centre
will be able to meet a double requirement:

'I know what it means: I mean what I say'.

Reviewing Your Own Development Needs

It would not be sensible to repeat all the exercises offered throughout the
book enabling manager developers to look at themselves before they look at
others. Instead, individuals could review themselves briefly against the
following exercise.

EXERCISE 12.2   PRIORITIES IN DEVELOPING MYSELF

The sequence suggested in this book for helping the development of someone
else can be used in assessing your own development needs.

Content Sequence
1. Are the requirements in my job – content, performance criteria, skills
    requirements – clear to me? (Chapters 1,2,3)
2. What kind of opportunities to learn exist within and around my job?
    (Chapter 3)
3. What is my understanding of effective ways of learning – the Learning
    Cycle and Learning Styles? (Chapter 4)
4. What is meant by help? (Chapter 5)
5. Who is there who might help in my personal development? (Chapter 6)
6. What skills do I need in order to help others, and what skills do I see
    employed by others in helping me? (Chapters 7, 8)
7. What opportunities are there available for me in learning from groups?
    (Chapter 8)
8. What kind of opportunities to learn exist through formal management
    development? (Chapters 9, 10)
9. What is my reaction to being helped? (Chapter 11)

Questions
1. Which of those issues carries greatest potential weight in looking at this
    moment at my development needs?
2. Do I need to revisit the relevant chapter in order to assess my
    development needs against that particular theme?
3. Which of the chapters or exercises has had the most impact on me in
    terms of recognizing my own development needs?

Principle of Reciprocity

In the Introduction, five reasons were given to explain why managers help develop others:

- they pursue the resolution of problems and in the process accidentally aid the development of others
- they believe improving the performance of others will reflect favourably on their own individual performance and perhaps also create more space for their own managerial interests and ambitions
- they derive satisfaction from helping someone to grow
- they develop their own skills and insight and knowledge as a result of sharing experiences with others
- their organization demands that they do.

It was suggested that the benefit of developing other people is going to be experienced by improvements in their performance. This is likely to be reflected in a reduction of problems that the more senior manager needs to handle, and a general improvement in performance in the unit for which the helping manager is responsible.

In terms of self-development, the possible creation of 'space' for the manager developer's own agenda is especially relevant. One of the consequences of reducing the number of problems or difficulties created by more junior managers is that helping managers are given eventually more time and space in which to develop their own skills and knowledge – often by pushing out the boundaries of their existing jobs.

'I put some time initially into coaching, problem solving and generally talking things through with my people. I sent several of them on courses but spent a lot of time in and around work here with them. It was time I sometimes grudged giving, and one or two of my colleagues thought that I was foolish to invest it in other people instead of doing things myself. But eventually I benefited, because they started to handle their own things better, I was able to delegate more and I could look around for more interesting and stretching work for myself. So, in the end, developing them created the opportunity for me to develop myself.'

The idea therefore that you get something back as a result of helping others is one version of the Principle of Reciprocity. Another, perhaps even more valuable version of it, is centred on the idea of equivalence of exchange. Whereas in the example above the helping manager is benefiting in the long term, there is no conscious reciprocity. It is possible to see yourself as being engaged in a process in which giving and receiving have greater equivalence. You may be giving to a younger, less experienced person from knowledge and experience, but they may be giving to you higher levels of energy and adventurousness.

Another kind of reciprocity could be called cognitive reciprocity. This is another version of the point made earlier about the relevance of undertaking the exercises and activities suggested in this book. Understanding the opportunities available to others, their possible feelings about them, and the ways in which they might be helped, gives a return to you in your understanding of your own situation, and potential for your own development.

Finally, for at least some individuals, the Principle of Reciprocity expresses itself through a very personal engagement. The pleasure of helping provides a different quality of feeling about what is given to, and what is received, by whom.

'I cannot describe to you how I felt when I saw him handle that very difficult negotiation, using some of the questions and tactics we had discussed. The difference from how he handled a previous negotiation was dramatic. I was thrilled at seeing the results of our preparation – but it was not pleasure in how clever I had been, it was satisfaction about what he was able to do. I felt as good about that as I did about the financial results – perhaps better.'

EXERCISE 12.3 THE PRINCIPLE OF RECIPROCITY

1. Review the five reasons why managers help develop others.
2. Assess each of them in the light of your experiences before reading this book. Mark each on a scale 0 = no importance, 10 = highly important.
3. Which have been the most important as motivators of your previous involvement in helping others?
4. Review the five reasons again. Would you change the scores now, in the light of what you have read in this book, or some other recent experience?

Seeking Help for Yourself

The solitary process of doing the exercises in this book is valuable but unlikely to be sufficient. All managers who, by definition, are in a position to help others develop, are also in a position to look for help from others. (The one exception is the chairman or equivalent person at the top of an organization, who has no superior to whom to turn. Such individuals will need to turn outside the organization for help.)

Once developers have completed for themselves the exercises or their selection of the exercises in this book, in pursuit of their own development, they should consider how they can obtain help from other people. They may already have developed the answer to this in undertaking Exercise 6.1 on page 83 of Chapter 6. If not, it is suggested that they complete that exercise now.

EXERCISE 12.4

1. Which of the individuals mentioned in Chapter 6 could be helpful in my own self-development?

2.   What opportunities or situations do I see arising in which one of the individuals mentioned might be more helpful than another?
3.   How could I best approach them for help? Is there a formal opportunity, e.g. appraisal or performance review, or do I need to seize an accidental chance?
4.   Have I considered the skills a potential developer actually has?
5.   Do those skills and/or styles of behaving relate to the way in which I would feel able to accept help?
6.   What action plan can I develop as a result of responding to the questions above?

Developers Helping Each Other

If other people in the developer's organization are similarly going through the kind of practices and techniques suggested in this book, then the individual developer can look for help from them in several different ways. Perhaps most obviously in relation to the content of this book, they can:

- discuss their experiences in trying to help others
- review the situations and individuals involved
- consider the causes of success or failure
- decide further action.

Perhaps more fundamentally from the point of view of many managers, they can be a source of information, advice and experience on a much wider range of managerial activities and managerial requirements. Help can, however, always be based on exchanging information and ideas: feedback from meetings that you have attended, discussions about particular problems, suggestions on how to handle difficult situations. The suggestion, therefore, that individuals should seek help from others in assessing and improving their activities in helping to develop others is the gateway to the much larger field of securing help on a much wider range of activities.

Managing Your Own Development Activities

Throughout this book, the emphasis has been on the use of real managerial work with its imperatives, priorities, disasters and successes as the driving force for development. It has been emphasized also that the development process is a management process – with defined objectives, results and requirements for monitoring performance. Any proposal of this kind to manage the development of others must similarly be applied to developers managing their self-development. Therefore they need to establish some goals, standards and methods of defining the end results. In Chart 12.1 there is an example, directed to the particular theme of this book.

Chart 12.1   Managing self-development

Goal
To be seen as a credible role model of self-development, in order to facilitate the development of others.

Standards
I will ask at the end of each weekly management meeting what the main learning experiences have been for us in the situations under review.

I will always offer my own comments but at the end of everyone else's contribution.

I will keep a management diary on the most significant events in which I am involved.

I will make reference to my entries in this diary wherever possible in order to persuade others of the benefits of a diary.

I will set up some specific learning activities for myself (? customer visit, courses) and report on them to my management team.

More Ideas on Self-Development

Since the purpose of this book is to describe the role of the manager developer, this chapter is short. The intention has been to show how offering help can interact in terms of facilitating the development of the developer as well as the learner, and to use some of the ideas in this book to provide a basis for the work necessary. The theme of self-development is a much larger one than is covered here. More detailed suggestions on what is involved and how to undertake it are given in Further Reading.

13

Towards the learning organization

There have been six main themes in this book:

- that the contribution of managers to the development of other managers must be based firmly on the reality of managerial work itself;
- that formally organized learning and informal or accidental learning have to be integrated through real work;
- that the nature of a learning process, once properly recognized, is fundamentally aligned to real managerial work – the Learning Cycle and Task Cycle coincide;
- that help is defined by the learner, not the developer;
- that the skills of the manager developer can be enhanced;
- that the interaction between developer and learner is one of reciprocal and not one-way benefit.

If the helping manager achieves a successful co-existence of these six themes, the door opens to an even more exciting prospect: managing more effectively managerial help in developing individuals, and then of groups, offers the chance of creating a learning organization.

Managing Help for the Individual

Improved development for individuals can be the effective base for growing the capacity of the organization, because the processes described here are centred in the organization, not played out on the periphery. For this to happen, the process as a whole must be managed.

Managing Development

If we enable managers to see the helping process as being not only about management but centred fundamentally on it, we are more likely to achieve the desirable goal of eliminating a conceptual and perceptual problem about management development. We need to enable managers to give more emphasis to helping others learn and develop while still not presenting them with a collection of beliefs, techniques, methodologies which persuade them that development and management are fundamentally different. The process of helping the development of others is a part of management in the same sense that at particular times a manager devotes attention to using management accounts, making a decision about a service or product, or selecting a candidate for a job. It is true that the development process can, for some individuals, also contain issues of values about people not necessarily related to performance. The problem arises for many managers when professional developers insist that the process should be largely driven by humanistic values of the development of the whole person, thereby persuading many managers that this is an abnormal process, an optional extra to be taken on if they happen to believe in the humanistic values being propagated. Managers should rather understand that the activity of helping others to develop is worthwhile because it provides direct and measurable managerial results, while for some it may contain the additional benefit of developing a person for more than managerial tasks.

The processes suggested in this book, therefore, are initiated and described not only through managerial work as usable development opportunities, but through managerial work on managing the development process. Carrying out the helping process effectively requires the helping managers to act in ways which are entirely familiar to them as managerial constructs. The elements are set out in Chart 13.1.

Chart 13.1   Managing the development process

- Understanding the context
- Setting objectives
- Defining required resources
- Setting out options
- Deciding what to do
- Planning actions
- Monitoring actions
- Evaluating results
- Providing rewards
- Planning the next steps

These elements, with one exception, have been discussed earlier in the book. The exception is 'providing rewards'. It is all too familiar in formal management development systems that apparently excellent systems are created on paper and announced with great fanfare, which either then fade gently away or collapse with greater suddenness. Failure to see management development as a process to be managed is certainly a main reason, and within that the issue of rewards is significant. The proposition contained throughout this book is that developing others is not only a managerial responsibility, and one which can be built often in and around the job, but one which will bring managerial benefits often to the manager developer, especially when the developer is the boss. Developing others is an important way to gaining more opportunities for yourself. Logic and intrinsic rewards of this kind are not sufficient. There needs to be built in some formal attention to extrinsic rewards because managers do what they are rewarded for doing. Rewards must be based on clear objectives and plans. There have to be monitoring processes and, finally, an evaluation – otherwise rewards are based on accidental and subjective occurrences which will bring no benefit to the management development process.

In addition to benefits arising for the individual developer, therefore, which may exist in some combination of personal satisfaction and managerial benefit, there need to be some extrinsic rewards offered by the organization.

These can be provided where, for example, a grand boss is asked to comment as part of an appraisal process on the ability of a subordinate to develop others. If performance on this issue is then subsequently taken into account on issues of promotion or, even more explicitly, of financial reward, then an organization begins to reach the position of rewarding effective development through the kind of extrinsic satisfiers that it provides for other aspects of management.

If organizations attempt to provide for appraisal by subordinates of their bosses, and not just the other way round, then similarly such appraisals can contain questions about the capacity of the boss as developer. Again, the reward system of the organization can take data from this kind of system into account.

It is possible to see, as just illustrated, how the developmental responsibility of bosses can and should be used in issues of performance review, Succession Planning and financial rewards. It is less easy to see how more voluntary processes can be rewarded. In the United States, attempts have been made to introduce awards such as 'Mentor of the Month'. It is not clear how successful such attempts have been. Again, the more obvious and appropriate process is to include in a performance review the success of an individual in mentoring someone else, even though that mentoring may not have been one of the main objectives or priorities in the mentor's main job.

An example of the steps which need to be undertaken is provided by TSB Retail Banking in the UK. They are attempting to raise the value of continuous learning by 'introducing more formal reward and recognition mechanisms such as awards for, say, best coach or best learner of the year'.

It is only when organizations define assisting the development of others as an element important enough to be assessed and contribute to the future of the manager developer within the organization that the development process will really become embedded in the managerial culture.

EXERCISE 13.1   MANAGING THE DEVELOPMENT PROCESS

Review Chart 13.1.

1. On a scale 10 = I am effective at this, 0 = I am not very effective at this, how would you rate your own performance, in managing your own development?
2. On a scale 10 = I am effective at this, 0 = I am not very effective at this, how would you rate your own performance in managing the development of others?
3. On a scale 10 = I am effective at this, 0 = I am not very effective at this, how would you rate the performance of your manager in managing the development of:

    a) yourself
    b) others?

4. On a scale 10 = I am effective at this, 0 = I am not very effective at this, how would you rate the performance of your organization as a whole in managing development?

A SWOT Analysis

The possibility of using a Strengths, Weaknesses, Opportunities, Threats Analysis as a contributor to defining management development needs was described in Chapter 10. My colleague, Gordon Wills, has suggested that this idea could be extended to broader issues of management development. I am grateful to him for permission to extend his original idea, in the form shown in Exercise 13.2. This is one route to defining how effective an organization is as a learning system.

EXERCISE 13.2   A SWOT ANALYSIS

My version of Gordon Wills's idea of extending a SWOT Analysis to a SWOT Learning Review is:

1. What learning system do we have in place emphasizing learning within and through the job?
2. How effective have those systems been over the last 12 months?
3. What learnings demonstrate that effectiveness in meeting opportunities or threats?

4.   What will be the main opportunities to learn over the next 12 months?
5.   What is likely to threaten the use of learning opportunities?

The Learning Organization

At the beginning of this chapter, it was stated that the themes and particular activities suggested throughout this book would contribute not only to the development of individuals but to the development of a Learning Organization.

The definition offered by myself and Peter Honey of the Learning Organization was given on page 77 in Chapter 5, and is repeated here in Chart 13.2.

Chart 13.2   Definition of the Learning Organization

'Creating an environment where the
behaviours and practices involved in
continuous development are actively encouraged'
(Peter Honey and Alan Mumford, 1991)

There are other definitions:

- Mike Pedler and his colleagues: 'An organisation which facilitates the learning of all its members and continually transforms itself'.
- Peter Senge: 'Organisations where people continually expand their capacity to create the results they desire, where new and expansive patterns of thinking are nurtured, where collective aspiration is set free, and where people are continually learning how to learn together'.

It will be noted that a difference between the Honey and Mumford definition and the others is the emphasis on 'behaviours and practices'. In our Learning Diagnostic Questionnaire, as illustrated in Chapter 5, we provide a means of assessing performance on these behaviours and practices. Thus we start with the individual's perception of what 'the organization' is doing to help development.

For any of these definitions of the Learning Organization to be met, the activities spelt out in this book are fundamental. As Senge says, 'Individual learning does not guarantee organisational learning, but without it no organisational learning occurs'. The shift from improved attention to the individual learner to achievement of the wider growth suggested in the concept of a Learning Organization will occur when four practices are put in place:

- Learning has to be central to the management process, not adopted as it so frequently is as an activity external to the management process – especially through activities away from real work.

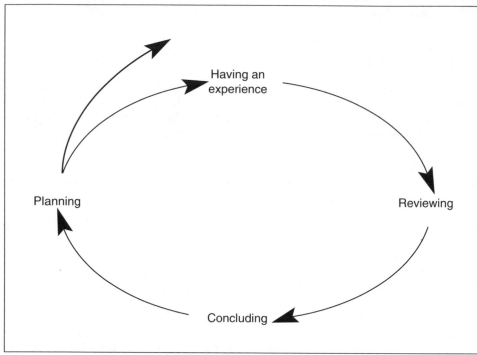

Figure 13.1   The Progressive Learning Cycle

- The processes and procedures necessary to encourage learning from and within the management process must be led by managers themselves. They have to take the lead because it is their direct involvement in normal work activities which facilitates the recognition of the opportunity and need to learn, in order to manage more effectively. Managers must also take the lead in identifying those formal management development processes which may be additionally effective in meeting skill or knowledge requirements which cannot be drawn from existing work practices.
- Learning has to be recognized as the continuous process it is, not a contrived series of special experiences. This can be recognized either through the Progressive Learning Cycle (Figure 13.1) or through a connected spiral of Learning Cycles.
- It is managers who must take the lead in adopting a regular procedure for reviewing the totality of the managerial work shared between themselves, their subordinates and their colleagues in order to introduce, at least improvements, and probably in many cases a vision of a transformed future.

The organization as a sensing, thinking being operating in learning mode must be driven by the concern of managers for managerial improvement

It is this prime concern which, if properly harnessed and directed, will lead to the adoption of those desirable learning practices and procedures which, built into the normality of managerial review processes rather than into the abnormality of so many formal management development schemes, will lead us in turn to the Learning Organization of the future.

Appendix

The role of the professional adviser

This Appendix is not designed to instruct the reader on how to be a professional trainer, developer, educator. Although some of the points made are certainly of general application, its purpose is to suggest how the professional adviser can make use of the material in this book.

Alternative Strategies

There are four different strategies for using this book. They are set out in Chart A.1.

Chart A.1   Strategies for the adviser

- Whole System
- Part System
- Opportunistic
- Personal

Whole System

At the peak of the success of the Peters and Waterman book, *In Search of Excellence*, some organizations gave a copy to all their managers. The intention presumably was to expose everyone to the ideas. One of the weaknesses of the method, as I found in subsequent research, was that there was rarely any attempt to follow up the book and to suggest what should be done as a result of reading it.

197

Since the case argued here is that all managers can and should provide help in the development of their subordinates, then giving a copy of the book to all managers would be in itself a way of highlighting this responsibility as well as, more usefully, providing managers with ways of carrying out the responsibility that is being highlighted. If this strategy is adopted, the adviser ought to make sure that:

- a reason for sending the book out is given
- links to existing management development policies and procedures are identified
- priorities are suggested – certain chapters may have resonance in particular organizations, units or with individuals
- suggestions are offered on what managers should do after reading the book – such as group discussions, how to experiment at an individual level
- a plan is set out for monitoring the impact of the book and results achieved from using it.

Part System

The book could be given to managers as a support for parts of the management development system:

- it could be included as reading material as part of a general management course, or a specific course on management development
- it could be used as a working resource as part of a course for mentors or coaches
- it could be given as a resource to go with guidance on how to conduct performance review and appraisal where there is a development plan requirement
- it could be used as a resource to go with the production of Personal Development Plans, Learning Contracts or Learning Agreements
- it could be used to assist with the production of required material for the Accreditation of Prior Learning or Crediting Competence processes for managerial qualifications.

Opportunistic

The adviser might look for development opportunities arising in the organization and recommend the book to managers involved in those activities. It could be recommended reading for a manager who is deploying individuals on a task group with learning possibilities – or on projects/ working parties with similar aims. This is the field in which there is so much scope, as demonstrated in the early chapters of this book, and of which unfortunately all too often the adviser is unaware. For this strategy to work effectively the adviser needs to be constantly in touch with a wide number of managers to take advantage of immediate opportunities. In addition, there are opportunities to be identified from the more formal management development process discussed in Chapters 9 and 10.

Personal

The Personal strategy involves use of the book through individuals rather than through activities. They may be individuals formally identified as mentors or coaches but who have not been on a course for this role. The book could be given to them, either as a standard resource to help them carry out their role or as a resource suggested for individuals who might be interested in reading the material.

The strategies are not necessarily alternatives to each other. The total coverage strategy suggested by the Whole System could, of course, be supported further through any of the other strategies. The great virtue of all these strategies other than Whole System is that they respond more to needs, rather than to an overall prescription. The clearest expression of this is obviously with the Opportunistic and Personal strategies, where an adviser would be responding to, or making use of, a clearly identified requirement by individual managers. These two strategies depend a great deal on the time and effort an adviser is prepared or able to devote to pursuing individual cases.

The choice of strategy ought to be determined by:

- the adviser's awareness of organizational opportunities, e.g. a project being set up
- the adviser's view of the organizational culture, e.g. is it likely to favour a 'Whole System' strategy
- the adviser's identification of units or individuals who might be specially interested
- the adviser's personal priorities, e.g. on the kind of work she or he wants to do
- the adviser's skills and likely level of influence.

EXERCISE A.1

1. Which of the above strategies seems most appropriate for you in your organization?
2. What are the positive forces that might encourage the implementation of your preferred strategy, and what are the negative forces that might restrict it?
3. Is there any past history of attempts to encourage managers to help

develop others? How does that history influence the likely implementation of your preferred strategy?
4.   How does your chosen strategy, or combination of strategies, relate to
your existing overall management development policy and strategy?

Self-Development – The Adviser as Role Model

The list of reasons identified in Chapter 12, setting out why manager
developers should undertake these actions for themselves before offering
help to others, applies equally to advisers:

- to establish experience in the opportunities and problems opened out by
the approaches suggested
- confirmation of validity of the ideas
- ability to respond from their own experience to questions about the ideas,
in a way which gives credibility.

There is a further reason which is partly identified by the phrase 'physician
heal thyself', and perhaps revealed more starkly by Chris Argyris's analysis of
the difference between Espoused Theory versus Theory in Use. His research
over many years has shown the extent to which managers declare belief in a
set of principles but then consistently behave according to another set of
principles or theories. In the context of this book the requirement is that
advisers should not only espouse belief in the primary role of the manager as
developer, but should behave according to that belief. If the management
development system proclaims belief in development through the job, do the
work priorities of the adviser reflect this – or instead a practice of running
courses? The extent to which an adviser will want to undertake every exercise
in the book will be determined by whether the whole book is to be used as a
resource by others. It is then desirable that advisers can respond to questions
on any part of it, not simply by giving explanations of what they think the
words mean, or why a particular exercise is desirable in principle, but also by
illustrating from their own experience wherever possible. If only part of the
book is to be used, then it is only *absolutely* necessary to cover the relevant
exercises.
Of course, not all advisers have managerial responsibility for others, not all
of them will be acting as a mentor, though most will probably have acted as
coach in some form or other. The important point is that they should be able
to show that, wherever credibility would be aided by their own completion of
the exercises, and this is possible, they have done so. Line managers are quite
rightly critical of advisers who recommend processes which they have not
applied to themselves.
While we need to accept the realities of particular advisers' jobs and
responsibilities, which may limit the potential for applying the exercises to
themselves, we need to recognize another limitation. The book has very

deliberately been presented at a level of analysis, commitment and understanding thought appropriate to line managers. This involves a recognition that managers are busy people capable of being persuaded by something practical and, at least in the UK, often not immediately persuadable or influenced by deeper, especially more emotional, issues. This means the book is very little concerned with some of the larger issues of life and personal growth and development. Professional advisers may have a greater interest in, a greater need to work on, and more knowledge and skills to implement self-development activities at deeper personal levels. They may well wish to consider offering advice to managers more geared to these issues, and may therefore want to find material for themselves and potentially for use with others in those areas not covered by this book.

Another aspect of depth, distinct from psychological and emotional aspects of development, was touched on in Chapter 11. It was suggested there that useful help would most often by defined as incremental, i.e. moving by small steps, rather than transformational, i.e. taking leaps. In that chapter, the point was being made in relation to Learning Style preferences, but the general issue of steps rather than leaps applies to the kind of strategy and advice to be presented by the adviser on all the aspects of this book. It may, for example, be entirely appropriate to discuss learning in terms of where manager helpers actually are, as what Argyris calls single loop learning, instead of aiming more ambitiously at double loop or transformational learning (see Further Reading).

Two further cautionary notes are necessary. The most obvious is that processes and objectives appropriate for the personal development of the adviser may be inappropriate for the line manager. As suggested earlier, the amount of time that an adviser might properly devote to personal development, because that ought to be the core of the job, is different from that which a line manager might sensibly be influenced to undertake. It is, however, not just a question of time, but of relative sophistication and the kind of language which professional developers use amongst themselves. The processes used by consenting developers in private are not necessarily appropriate to a less sophisticated managerial population.

The second cautionary note is that advisers need to look to their level of skills and experience before offering help. Since the book is geared to the perceived capacity of line managers to handle the exercises involved, there should be no problem for advisers who will be more aware of what is involved at the level at which the book operates. But in the deeper and more sensitive areas not covered here, advisers certainly ought to review the extent to which they have the professional capability to operate.

Helping Developers – Some Illustrative Questions

Whatever the strategy chosen by the adviser, questions will arise from individual managers. They will arise because the management development system generates them or because the managerial situation produces them. Here are some typical questions:

- 'I have to do the last page of the appraisal form, on recommendations for training and development. I find this very difficult to fill in for a number of my people. They have been on all the relevant courses. What else can I do for them?'
- 'I have put Anne on a task force to look at the pros and cons of having an open plan office. She was very pleased, and said she saw it as a good opportunity to work with some new people and develop some of her skills. Frankly I had not thought of that as one of the factors – I just put her on it to represent a point of view. What sort of learning do you think might be involved, and is there anything I should be doing about it?'
- 'I have read this note you have sent me on the preparation I should go through before Steven goes on the Interpersonal Skills courses I have nominated him for. Your note says that before he goes I should discuss with him his needs in detail, so he can concentrate on this during the course, and then talk to me afterwards on how it has helped him. I just thought his interpersonal skills could do with some polishing. What else am I expected to say to him?'
- 'I have just come back from the General Management course. There was some interesting material, very realistic, by Mintzberg and Kotter, on networking. It impressed me, but I think a number of my people could also benefit from understanding this. It's a question of how you can learn from the people around you. They can't all go on the course. How could I convey the idea to them so that I can help them use their network contacts more effectively?'
- 'I think John Jones needs to be better equipped to handle management accounts in preparation for the next job we have lined up for him. Is there a course I can send him on, or some other way we can give him what he needs?'
- 'Now that we have done Quality Circles and Team Building, the OK words are mentoring and coaching. I'm not sure what the difference is between a boss, a mentor and a coach. Does it matter?'

A list of questions of this kind is infinitely extendable. Here are some ways in which this book assists with potential responses to such questions.

EXERCISE A.2   MANAGERIAL QUESTIONS TO THE ADVISER

1. Review the list of questions above. Can you add one or more from your experience relevant to the issues discussed in this book?
2. Which of the examples given above, supplemented by your own experiences, highlights the most important issue to you on Helping the Manager Developer?
3. Which chapters of the book are most relevant to that question?

4. How would you use the book in responding to the question?
5. How would you monitor the effectiveness of any advice you give?

Types of Help

The material suggested earlier for the identification by manager developers of the criteria for effective help also apply to the adviser. They derive from the principle that help is defined by the person who wants the help, not by the helper. (Remember also, the point made earlier about the level and sophistication of advice to be offered.) When pursuing personal strategies, an awareness of the characteristics and interests of the individual to be advised is likely to facilitate effective help. The adviser should therefore certainly undertake the exercises in Chapter 12, amending them where necessary to suit the situation of the adviser rather than the line manager.

Advisers will have different responsibilities, depending on their organizational situation, and the procedures within the management development system, and through managerial incidents and personal opportunities. Of the helping roles specified at the beginning of this book, the roles of coach, mentor and colleague are relevant to carrying out the adviser role. The roles of boss, grand boss, subordinate and client are not in the adviser role. These latter four roles, while themselves providing clearly opportunities for giving help, differ because the adviser is then acting as a line manager, not as an adviser.

One helpful way of looking at the different types of help an adviser may offer is shown in Chart A.2.

Chart A.2 Types of help by advisers

- System Instruction
- System Tutoring
- Personal Coaching
- Personal Counselling

System Instruction

The adviser may be called on to provide assistance such as:

- writing the management development policy, devising the strategy planning the use of resources
- specifically, setting up 'managers developing managers' processes
- responding to questions such as 'what course can you recomm

'what do these words in the book/guidance note/personal development form actually mean?'
* monitoring and evaluating the results of 'managers developing managers' processes.

System Tutoring

This is the more direct and individual role, for example, in running courses on Personal Development, Managers Developing Managers, Appraisal, Personal Development Plans, Learning Contracts. On all of these, the adviser may be the direct provider or may be the intermediary who decides on the use of an external resource.

Personal Coaching

Coaching gives advisers the opportunity to give direct help to individuals or to a group. In relation to this book, it is the process by which individuals would be helped to select and make use of exercises from it. Of course, advisers will generate their own opportunities and processes as well, all directed at helping the manager developer carry out the tasks of diagnosis, opportunity recognition, coaching and mentoring. It will often be a response to a specific question: 'I want to set up a learning review at a management meeting. I am not sure how best to do it. For example, Simon will be keen and Jean won't be'.

Personal Counselling

The difference between the terms 'coaching' and 'counselling' is not always very clear. One interpretation is that coaching is concerned with the development of skills, whereas counselling addresses wider issues. Counselling will often precede coaching because it identifies the issues on which coaching might be required. Examples of questions leading to counselling include:

* 'One of my people consistently irritates other people. I would like to talk to you about what happens and what I might do about it.'
  'I have been reading the chapters from this book you recommended. To which of my people would you think I should best apply it?'
  'Should I behave differently when I'm coaching from when I'm discussing problem?'

An adviser may be required to use all of these different types of help. Different line managers might require help in one type but not another. Sometimes, of course, a manager might be given help through all four types over a period of time. It is important for the adviser to recognize the type of help appropriate to the situation and to the individual. In addition, it is well worth considering what proportion of an adviser's work is spent on which type. Many advisers devote most of their time to offering system instruction or system tutoring help. They should at least consider whether more effort devoted to personal coaching and personal counselling would be more appropriate either for their priorities within the organization as a whole, or in relation to particular situations or individuals.

EXERCISE A.3 TYPES OF HELP

Review each of the four types.

1. Do you use all four types in your job?
2. Which type do you believe to be most effective?
3. What information do you have to support your conclusion?
4. What is the proportion of your time and energy that goes into each of the types?
5. Is there a case for changing the proportion of your time and energy devoted to each type?
6. How might you make the change?
7. What advice or help would you need from anyone else in order to decide on the change and to implement it?

Recognizing Problems with the Manager Developer

One of the characteristics of the Whole System strategy, and the types of help defined as System Instruction and System Tutoring, is that they imply that help is forced on managers. That is one of the reasons why the strategy and type must be carefully considered. The benefits to the line manager of taking further responsibility for, and implementing actions on, helping others to develop were identified in the Introduction and extended in Chapter 12. Some managers may identify strongly with a performance benefit, others with a more general interest in developing people. Not all will take up the challenge willingly or effectively. These are often general issues about management development not unique to the ideas expressed in this book. The specific features of unwillingness relevant to this book are:

Lack of priority: Despite the statement about benefits, advisers will be faced with managers who say that their priority is to get work done, not to develop other people.

Failure to make conceptual leaps: A large part of this book is concerned with translating real managerial work into development opportunities. While for many managers this translation is easily explained and accepted, some managers find the concept extraordinarily difficult to grasp.

Impatience: The relatively thoughtful, rational, planned, reflective practices suggested here can be dismissed by some managers. 'I simply don't have time', or 'People will make their own way without all this input from me'.

Insecurity: Some managers are fearful about the consequences of developing other people to a level of skill equivalent to their own. Or they may be concerned that developing an individual will only lead to that individual departing for another job somewhere else.

Hopelessness: 'People are what they are. You can't really make much of them. Managers are born not made.'

Over-dependence: A quite different sort of problem, often not recognized by advisers for some time. Some managers become very interested and involved, but constantly resort to the adviser for further help. 'Can you sit in at my meeting with Susan?' 'I would like you to have a chat with John; I have done his appraisal and drawn up a learning agreement with him but I would like you to go over things as well.' What may at first be exciting opportunities for the adviser, and implicit acceptance of his/her skill and potential to contribute may, if prolonged, become a situation in which the manager is over-dependent on the adviser.

EXERCISE A.4   RECOGNIZING PROBLEMS WITH THE MANAGER DEVELOPER

Consider the managers with whom you will be working in introducing the ideas reviewed in this book.

1.   Are there significant groups, or individuals, with whom some of these problems exist?
2.   How significant are the groups or individuals?
3.   How significant are the problems?
4.   What action have you taken so far to try to reduce the problems?
5.   What actions might you take in future?

Getting Help from Others

Advisers will need to pay special attention to their own response to Chapter 12 – Develop Yourself; the main suggestions in that chapter are not repeated here, although a few points are worth emphasizing. For most managers and advisers solitary learning is a difficult process. Advisers need to look at a variety of sources of help in learning how to advise on the issues presented in this book. The most solitary form of learning is reading, and Further Reading provides suggestions on this. Advisers should set aside some reading time in their diaries. If they do not do this, most of them will be unlikely to do the reading. It will be sensible for many advisers then to check the results of their reading with colleagues.

The other form of solitary learning is to keep a Learning Log, or find some other way of regularly reviewing learning.

Other forms of exchange replicate those offered to managers in this book. Chart A.3 indicates the possibilities.

Chart A.3   Helpers and their roles

	Problem solving	Coaching	Mentoring	Counselling	Performance review and needs	Manager in dev. system	Learning to learn
Grand boss	X	X	–	X	X	X	X
Boss	X	X	–	X	X	X	X
Mentor	X	X	X	X	–	½	X
Colleague	X	½	X	X	?	–	?
Subordinate	X	–	–	–	–	–	?
Project client	½	–	–	–	X	–	–
Self	X	?	?	?	X	X	X

EXERCISE A.5   ADVISERS NEED HELP TOO!

Advisers should review Chart A.3.

1. Who has been most helpful to you in your personal development?
2. Who could be most helpful to you on the issues, techniques and opportunities discussed in this book?
3. How might you approach them?
4. Will the Principle of Reciprocity operate – what can you offer them?
5. What form of help would be most helpful to you?

An interesting structured mentoring process for advisers has been set up at Roffey Park Management College. Under the guidance of Ian Cunningham, the Chief Executive, all new tutors are asked to choose a mentor from among their colleagues. In addition, the mentors meet as a group to discuss their experiences as mentors.

Measuring Results

Of course, advisers ought to be monitoring and evaluating the success of all the management development systems, policies and procedures with which they are involved. Advisers ought to undertake monitoring and evaluation in relation to what they have done as a result of reading this book.

EXERCISE A.6   EVALUATING RESULTS

1.   How did I attempt to use the book?
2.   How successful was I?
3.   What helped me and what hindered me in achievements on this?
4.   How have I tried to integrate this with other management development processes?
5.   What parts of the organization or individuals could I propose as exemplars or centres of excellence?
6.   How might I use them?
7.   What have I learned from what I have attempted to do?
8.   What actions will I take as a result of this review?

Actions for the Adviser

The vogue amongst trainers for setting behavioural objectives to be met by individuals attending courses which emerged in the 1960s and 1970s has been challenged in more recent years. Desirable though it seems for trainers to be clear about what they are trying to achieve, there is a conflict with the self-development philosophy which says that individuals set their own goals to meet their own needs. In the same way, this section could be challenged by some readers, because it sets out the author's view on actions which should be undertaken. With that warning, which should enable any individual who wants to produce his or her own list of actions to do so, Chart A.4 is offered as being generally helpful to many advisers.

A Final Word – Reassurance

Much of this book has been centred on providing help in real work situations. The suggestion is that advisers could spend more time advocating, illustrating and working through the exercises in this book with manager developers. As the options at the beginning of this Appendix show, this advice might be given off the job as part of a course, or more selectively to individuals in the work context.

Advisers have sometimes expressed concern to me about the implied shift in their priorities. As the exercises in this Appendix indicate, a review of the appropriate priorities is certainly desirable. However, no adviser needs to worry that a shift of priorities to give more attention to manager developers will 'lead to the death of the management development system we have spent painful years building up'. The suggestions in this book enable manager developers to do what they are best placed to do. The adviser retains the primary professional role of producing suggestions for the design of the management development system and strategies (see Further Reading).

Chart A.4   Actions for the adviser

Action 1: What are the most important things you should do as an adviser as a result of reading this book? (The implication is that advisers should have undertaken most if not all of the exercises themselves.)

Action 2: Set out your views on your job, your priorities and the skills you need in order to undertake the work suggested in this chapter. What action do you need to take to improve your skills and experience for the issues covered in this book?

Action 3: Discuss the results of Action 2 with your boss and seek agreement on priorities and development actions for yourself.

Action 4: Decide which of the chapters in the book most interest you. Then decide which are most likely to interest a client to whom you have access. Choose a group or an individual with whom to carry out some pilot work.

Action 5: Decide what action you can take in providing help to the developers. What is your strategy? What is your action plan to go with the strategy? Which of the four styles will be most appropriate in which proportion?

Action 6: How do the ideas in this book relate to your current management development system? How can they be integrated? Re-read all your internal management development literature on your policy, the system, Appraisal, Personal Development Plans, etc. Check every reference to the role of boss, coach and mentor. Review how far this book affects existing interpretations of these roles, and how far it might affect implementation. Look especially at how to integrate the formal system of management development with accidental learning opportunities.

Action 7: What action could you undertake to improve your present provision of Appraisal, Personal Development Plans, Learning Agreements?

Action 8: Assess the organizational climate in relation to the ideas presented in this book. Which of the ideas is most likely to be congruent with the organizational climate? Might it be favourable to a formal process of mentoring and coaching, or more likely to be attracted to Personal Development Plans?

Action 9: Review how you can get close to the customer and stay close to the action by helping the manager as developer. What opportunities exist or can be created for you to become more aware of learning opportunities in and around the job for other people.

Action 10: What does the corporate plan/business plan say on issues which might influence your strategy for implementing these ideas? Are there other business or organizational planning documents which might help provide reasons or situations? After that, look at what succession plans and other existing management development planning information provides.

Action 11: Who are the best managers as developers of managers in your organization? In which units are there the best systems or processes for encouraging others to learn. How might you use these individuals or units?

Further Reading

Managerial Work

R. Stewart, *Contrasts in Management*, McGraw-Hill, New York, 1976
H. Mintzberg, *The Value of Managerial Work*, Prentice-Hall, Englewood Cliff, NJ, New York, 1980

Managerial Work as Learning Opportunities

M.W. McCall, M.M. Lombardo and A.M. Morrison, *The Lessons of Experience*, Lexington Books, Lexington, Mass., 1988
A. Mumford, *Developing Top Managers*, Gower, Aldershot, 1988
A. Mumford, P. Honey, and G. Robinson, *Developing Directors: Making Experience Count*, Training Agency, Sheffield, 1990
P. Honey and A. Mumford, *Manual of Learning Opportunities*, Honey, Maidenhead, 1989
P. Honey and A. Mumford, *The Opportunist Learner*, Honey, Maidenhead, 1990
J. Gabarro, 'When a New Manager Takes Charge', *Harvard Business Review*, May–June 1985
L. Hill, *Becoming A Manager*, Harvard Business School Press, Boston, 1992
C. Handy, 'How To Learn From the Real Thing', *The Director*, June 1992

Learning, Self-Development and being Helped

D. Kolb, *Experiential Learning*, Prentice-Hall, Englewood Cliffs, NJ, New 1984
P. Honey and A. Mumford, *Manual of Learning Styles*, Honey, Ma: 3rd Edition, 1992

P. Honey and A. Mumford, *Using Your Learning Styles*, Honey, Maidenhead, 1986

P. Honey and A. Mumford, *Manual of Learning Opportunities*, Honey, Maidenhead, 1989

A. Morrison, R. White, and E. Van Velsor, *Breaking the Glass Ceiling*, Addison Wesley, 1987

E. Van Velsor, and M. W. Hughes, *Gender Differences in the Development of Managers: How Women Managers Learn from Experience*, Center for Creative Leadership, Greensboro, 1990

G. Hofstede, *Cultures and Organisations*, McGraw-Hill, Maidenhead, 1991

M. Pedler, J. Burgoyne, and T. Boydell, *A Manager's Guide to Self-Development*, McGraw-Hill, Maidenhead, 2nd Edition, 1986

A. Mumford, 'Self-Development: Missing Elements', *Industrial and Commercial Training*, **18** (3), 1986

M. Pedler, J. Burgoyne, T. Boydell and G. Welshman, *Self-Development in Organisations*, McGraw-Hill, Maidenhead, 1990

Managers as Developers

R. Horton, *What Works For Me*, Random House, New York, 1986

C. Margerison, *Making Management Development Work*, McGraw-Hill, Maidenhead, 1991

E. Kram and L. Isabella, 'Alternatives to Mentoring: The Role of Peer Relationships in Career Development', *Academy of Management Journal*, **28** (1), March 1985

D. Clutterbuck, *Everyone Needs a Mentor*, Institute of Personnel Management, Wimbledon, 2nd Edition, 1991

D. Megginson and T. Boydell, *A Manager's Guide to Coaching*, Bacie, London, 1979

D. Megginson, 'Instructor, Coach, Mentor: Three Ways of Helping for Managers', *Management Education and Development*, **19**, Part 1, 1988

A. Collin, 'Notes on Some Typologies of Management Development and the Role of the Mentor', *Personnel Review*, **8** (1), 1979

B. Smith, 'Mutual Mentoring on Projects', *Journal of Management Development*, **9** (1), 1990

K. Kram, 'Phases of the Mentor Relationship', *Academy of Management Journal*, **6** (4), 1983

L. Marsh, 'Good Manager: Good Coach', *Industrial and Commercial Training*, **24** (9), 1992

E. Parsloe, *Coaching, Mentoring and Assessing*, Kogan Page, London, 1992

D. Burdett, 'To Coach or Not to Coach That is the Question', *Industrial and Commercial Training* (Part 1) **23** (5), 1991, (Part 2) **23** (6), 1991

eary and D. Megginson, *The Line Manager as Developer*, Henley Distance ning Ltd, Henley, 1992

ld and M.J. Davidson, 'Adopt a Mentor – The New Way Ahead for Managers', *Women in Management Review*, **5** (1), 1990

Formal Management Development and Integrating Work-based Learning

C. Margerison, *Making Management Development Work*, McGraw-Hill, Maidenhead, 1991

G. McBeath, *Practical Management Development*, Blackwell, Oxford, 1990

A. Mumford, *Management Development: Strategies for Action*, Institute of Personnel Management, London, 2nd Edition, 1993

G. Boak, *Developing Managerial Competences: The Management Learning Contract Approach*, Pitman, London, 1991

Various publications by the Management Charter Initiative are available from Management Charter Initiative, Russell Square House, 10 Russell Square, London WC1B 5BR

The Learning Organization

M. Pedler, J. Burgoyne, and T. Boydell, *The Learning Company*, McGraw-Hill, Maidenhead, 1991

P. Senge, *The Fifth Discipline: The Art and Practice of the Learning Organisation*, Doubleday, New York, 1990

P. Honey and A. Mumford, *The Manual of Learning Opportunities*, Honey, Maidenhead, 1989

C. Argyris, 'Double Loop Learning in Organisations', *Harvard Business Review*, Sept–Oct 1977

C. Argyris, *Reasoning, Learning and Action*, Jossey-Bass, San Francisco, 1982

The Work of the Professional Adviser

C. Margerison, *Managerial Consulting Skills*, Gower, Aldershot, 1988

Association for Management Education and Development, *Developing the Developers*, London, 1991

E.H. Schein, *Process Consultation Vol. 2*, Addison-Wesley, 1987

C. Argyris, *Strategy, Change and Defensive Routine*, Pitman, 1985

G. Egan, *The Skilled Helper*, Brook Cole, 3rd Edition, 1986

A. Mumford, *Management Development: Strategies for Action*, Institute of Personnel Management, London, 1990

Index

The Goal

Beating the Competition

Second Edition

Eliyahu M Goldratt and Jeff Cox

Written in a fast-paced thriller style, *The Goal* is the gripping novel which is transforming management thinking throughout the Western world.

Alex Rogo is a harried plant manager working ever more desperately to try to improve performance. His factory is rapidly heading for disaster. So is his marriage. He has ninety days to save his plant - or it will be closed by corporate HQ, with hundreds of job losses. It takes a chance meeting with a colleague from student days - Jonah - to help him break out of conventional ways of thinking to see what needs to be done.

The story of Alex's fight to save his plant is more than compulsive reading. It contains a serious message for all managers in industry and explains the ideas which underlie the Theory of Constraints (TOC) developed by Eli Goldratt - the author described by Fortune as 'a guru to industry' and by Businessweek as a 'genius'.

As a result of the phenomenal and continuing success of *The Goal*, there has been growing demand for a follow-up. Eliyahu Goldratt has now written ten further chapters which continues the story of Alex Rogo as he makes the transition from Plant Manager to Divisional Manager. Having achieved the turnround of his plant, Alex now attempts to apply all that Jonah has taught him, not to crisis management, but to ongoing improvement.

These new chapters reinforce the thinking process utilised in the first edition of *The Goal* and apply them to a wider management context with the aim of stimulating readers into using the technique in their own environment.

| 1993 | 352 pages | 0 566 07417 6 Hardback | 0 566 07418 4 Paperback |

Gower

Problem Solving in Groups

Second Edition

Mike Robson

Modern scientific research has demonstrated that groups are likely to solve problems more effectively than individuals. As most of us knew already, two heads (or more) are better than one. In organizations it makes sense to harness the power of the group both to deal with problems already identified and to generate ideas for enhancing effectiveness by reducing costs, increasing productivity and the like.

In this revised and updated edition of his successful book, Mike Robson first introduces the concepts and methods involved. Then, after setting out the advantages of the group approach, he examines in detail each of the eight key problem solving techniques. The final part of the book explains how to present proposed solutions, how to evaluate results and how to ensure that the group process runs smoothly.

With its practical tone, its down-to-earth style and lively visuals, this is a book that will appeal strongly to managers and trainers looking for ways of improving their organization's and their department's performance.

Contents

1993   176 pages   0 566 07414 1 Hardback   0 566 07415 X Paperback

Gower

Building a Better Team
A handbook for
managers and facilitators

Peter Moxon

Team leadership and team development are central to the modern manager's ability to "achieve results through other people". Successful team building requires knowledge and skill, and the aim of this handbook is to provide both. Using a unique blend of concepts, practical guidance and exercises, the author explains both the why and the how of team development.

Drawing on his extensive experience as manager and consultant, Peter Moxon describes how groups develop, how trust and openness can be encouraged, and the likely problems overcome. As well as detailed advice on the planning and running of teambuilding programmes the book contains a series of activities, each one including all necessary instructions and support material.

Irrespective of the size or type of organization involved, Building a Better Team offers a practical, comprehensive guide to managers, facilitators and team leaders seeking improved performance.

Contents

1993   250 pages   0 566 07424 9

Gower

The People Side of Project Management

Ralph L Kliem and Irwin S Ludin

This book explains the inter-relationships among the major parties of a project and provides ways for project managers to ensure cooperative, harmonious relationships.

It is written for everyone in business working on a project, regardless of industry. It addresses the psychological and political gaps that affect the outcome of projects. Senior management, project managers, project team members, and clients will all benefit from this book, particularly in mid-size and large firms where the "people factor" plays an important role. The book will enhance a better understanding of the "ins and outs" of how major participants of projects think, relate, act and interact.

It identifies the major players in a project environment and discusses the relationships (referred to as the people side) that exist among them from the perspective of the project manager. It discusses the impact of these relationships, throughout the project lifecycle, on major project activities, such as planning, budgeting, change management, and monitoring. It also discusses how project managers can improve these relationships: topics include leading individual team members, motivating the entire team, dealing with the client, and dealing with senior management. Finally, it discusses the qualities of effective project managers that engender cooperative, harmonious relationships among project participants.

1993   200 pages   0 566 07363 3

Gower

Running an Effective Training Session

Patrick Forsyth
of
Touchstone Training and Consultancy

This down-to-earth guide to planning and delivering a training session will be welcomed by new and experienced trainers alike - as well as by line managers and other professionals with training responsibility. In his latest book Patrick Forsyth takes the reader step-by-step through the process of structuring the session and preparing materials, before covering the presentational techniques involved in detail. The final section is concerned with following up in terms of evaluation and establishing links to further training . The user-friendly text is supported throughout by examples.

For anyone involved in training, Patrick Forsyth's new book represents a painless way to improve performance.

Contents
Introduction • Establishing a basis • Planning the session • Preparing course materials • Running the session: presentational techniques • Running the session: participative techniques • Following up • Appendix: ready-to-use training material • Index

1992   142 pages   0 566 07320 X

Gower

A Systematic Approach to
Getting Results

Surya Lovejoy

Every manager has to produce results. But almost nobody is trained in the business of doing so. This book is a practical handbook for making things happen. And whether the something in question is a conference, an office relocation or a sales target, the principles are the same: you need a systematic approach for working out...

- exactly what has to happen
- when everything has to happen
- how you will ensure that it happens
- what could go wrong
- what will happen when something does go wrong
- how you will remain sane during the process

This book won't turn you into an expert on critical path analysis or prepare you for the job of running the World Bank. What it will do is to give you the tools you need to produce results smoothly, effectively, reliably and without losing your mind on the way.

Contents
Introduction • Turning a task into a project • Turning a project into an action plan • Creating and managing the budget • Creating project maps • Creating a winning team • Turning the action plan into action • Outwitting the paperwork • Remaining sane • Avoiding the technology trap • Crisis projects • Help! • After the project • Index.

1992   191 pages   0 566 07326 9

Gower

Assertiveness for Managers
Terry Gillen

Flatter organizations, decentralized authority, changing technology, obsolete skills, downsizing, retraining, outplacement - these are common features of today's business environment. Against such a background, success depends increasingly on the personal credibility of individual managers. In this timely book, *Terry Gillen* explains how an assertive style of management can dramatically improve effectiveness. He sets out the principles and benefits of assertive behaviour and shows how to apply assertiveness techniques in everyday management situations.

Part One places assertiveness in the context of the modern manager's job, illustrates the three main types of behaviour and describes a method of harnessing emotional energy to ensure the desired results.

Part Two shows how to handle a range of management problems, including aggressive bosses or colleagues, receiving/giving criticism, disciplining staff, resolving conflict and controlling stress. Each chapter contains examples of the particular problem, guidance on how to deal with it assertively and a summary for rapid reference.

Contents

1992   257 pages   0 566 02861 1

Gower